BOOTLEGGER

The Good, The Bad & The Tasty

Karl Phillips

with Peter Read and Iestyn Bryn Jones

This book is dedicated to Claire, Iwan, Mum, Dad and the friends that have stuck around.

Without them, it would've been ready much friggin' earlier!

First impression: 2022

The publishers wish to acknowledge the support
of the Books Council of Wales

Cover image: Dean Jones
Cover design: Tanwen Haf

ISBN: 978 1 912631 37 7

Published and printed in Wales
on paper from well-maintained forests by
Y Lolfa Cyf., Talybont, Ceredigion SY24 5HE
website www.ylolfa.com
e-mail ylolfa@ylolfa.com
tel 01970 832 304
fax 832 782

Contents

Foreword

I've been following this man's rise in popularity over the last few years 'n' couldn't have been happier when I heard he'd blagged a book deal! 'Top man' are the words that came to mind when the publishers approached me and asked me to write a Foreword.

Every time I look at his Twitter account, he has a few extra thousand followers. How does he do it? I've figured it out – it's no act, he's just himself. He's a natural.

I'm lucky enough to be one of the first people to have a read-through of this book and I can tell you now – you're gonna be spoilt. I thought that I'd lived a colourful life until I read about Karl's different adventures around Wales and beyond.

I'm glad this book's finally ready, 'cause now I might be asked to go on a book tour as one of Karl's guests. That drink is well overdue!

We've met up a few times over the years and I'm glad to say he's a nice guy – a genuine guy. The last time we met, I encouraged him not to change anything about himself as he gets more and more popular. Thousands of followers later, and he's the same ol' Karl. Now, more than ever, we need characters that give off good vibes.

There's enough bad news on the telly. Whenever I see him on Twitter or YouTube, he always cracks me up. As far as Wrexham legends go, it's a privilege to share some of the limelight with the Captain!

Mickey Thomas
January 2022

CHAPTER ONE

Early Doors

Here we go!

With just over 24 hours until kick-off, I'm excited – so excited that I've popped down to the Wheatsheaf Inn for a few pints to steady my nerves. I've got my camera with me and I start filming what's become one of my most popular videos (for the right and wrong reasons) on YouTube: Bootleggers MOTD (Chester v. Wrexham). I turn the camera onto myself and start: "Can you see me? Can you hear me? Over and owt," I say down the lens as I take a sip from my pint. "Who you talkin' to there?" says Pam, the delightful landlady. It's not just the barmaid that's laughing. A few of the lads are having a bit of a chuckle and a heckle too. "Here he goes again!" says one, as he looks across the bar. I have another sip of my pint and ask myself the question: "Who ARE you talkin' to Karl?" There's a lot happened to me since 2015. It turns out I've been talkin' to millions of people over the last few years... and I'm only just gettin' warmed up, baby!

I've gotta admit – the thought of writing this book has been meltin' my friggin' brain. But if I don't give this a duckin' shot, someone else will! So you're getting this straight from the Captain's mouth.

One thing before I get started: the stories I'm gonna share are my recollection of events. Some names, locations and characteristics have been changed to protect the privacy of those mentioned. Apart from the legal reasons, it's out of respect too. The dialogue has been recreated from my puddled memory. I've got a few sad, funny and cringeworthy stories. All in all, I want it to have a feel-good factor, so if you're reading this before bed, it'll warm you up a treat.

In the beginning...

I landed on this planet in Wrexham Maelor Hospital in October 1974. My mum would say I've been a "pain in the arse from day one!" We lived in Coedpoeth, a small village on the outskirts of Wrexham. It's a working-class village. I've got some good memories of the place.

My parents were about 16 when they had me. I don't know about you, but I couldn't even look after myself properly at 16, never mind a small child. When I was a toddler, my parents were given a flat on the High Street, above a clothes shop called Family Fashions. From what I've heard, times were a bit tough, but my dad – usually known as Turkey – tried his best to provide for his family. There are rumours that one of his party tricks was adapting a metal coat hanger so he could open the door into Family Fashions. I don't know if that's true, but if it was, I guess at least for a brief period, the Mini Captain was dressed quite sharply.

After the flat, my parents were lucky enough to get a council house at Heol Glyndwr. This is where I would live until my early teens. I remember there was no carpet on the stairs. The earliest sound that hit my ears was heavy metal, rocking its way through our walls. It came from a neighbouring house, a few doors down. The parents had about three sons and two daughters, and all of them seemed to love rock music. To be fair, they had good taste: they were into Iron Maiden, AC/DC, Deep Purple, Led Zep and Hendrix. I could hear the music bangin' away until late at night. And as I'd look out into the night sky, I'd sometimes see shady figures shuffling around in the dark: a cheeky snog, a shifty smoke, a blazing row or someone tryin' to syphon a milk bottle's worth of petrol out of Percy's Hillman Imp. There was always something to watch from my bedroom window. One thing I could see was a small patch of grass, which became my playground. I was good friends with a few of the Rawlinson and O'Keefe children, who lived nearby. Some would say I was a weird little kid. I was the one wearing the brown duffle coat, constantly talking to myself.

"That boy's not normal!" I'd hear people say about me.

"He looks like that little boy off *The Omen* film!" I also remember hearing.

I wouldn't have said I was weird. I was just different. And there's most definitely nothing wrong with being different. I'd be busy talkin' to myself, doin' the football commentary when we were all havin' a game of footy. I was always in my own little world and even developed my own language. After my mates went in for tea, I'd be bangin' the Mitre Delta footy against next door's hedge, doin' an impression of Brian Moore as a commentator.

In them days, it was a case of, "Get out of the house. I don't want to see you all day!" I'd spend my days with my mates. When we weren't playin' footy, we'd be Hedge Hopping. Hedge Hopping entailed hurdling over the hedgerows of several bungalows without getting lynched off one of the residents. Another favourite was Nick Nocking. We knew whose doors to knock for the best chase. It was a great laugh when you made your escape, but it was less fun when you had a pummelling. We'd spend the evenings singing the Band Aid song in the local bogs while some of the lads tried to spark up nippings they'd found by the bus stop. Deeew – back then there was a lot of smokin' goin' on. Bet Lynch would be walkin' into the Rovers with 40 fags in her handbag. You'd get on the bus and some ducker would be smokin'. No matter where you went, someone would be blowin' smoke rings.

The summer holidays seemed to last forever. The days seemed endless. Most of the lads I was hangin' about with were a bit older than me, so there was a later curfew for them. But woe betide me if I was ever home later than the agreed time. I'd be in for the slipper treatment. Deeew – you knew about it when you caught one of them. I remember catchin' a few.

One of the most memorable slipper treatments came when I found the Christmas presents Mum had stashed at the back of the wardrobe in her bedroom. I remember peepin' into the wardrobe and seeing the presents. I thought to myself, 'The older boys were right – there IS no such thing as Santa. It IS Mam that gets the presents!'

It was when I went back for a second inspection that I was caught. I was trying to figure out what the presents were – 'Are they for me or Trina (my younger sister)?' Then it came. WHACK. Deeew, it felt like I'd been stung by a swarm of bees. She was seething. My mum, like a lot of people back then, had been planning early.

Another childhood memory was my mum screaming every time she saw a spider. Jesus wept – that council house was full of 'em and there was plenty of marks on the walls where Mam had given them the slipper too.

The young Captain couldn't get enough of the telly and the Eighties was a glorious era for it. *Minder, Duty Free, Murder She Wrote* and *Magnum*. They simply do not make telly programmes like they did back then. Characters like Terry McCann and Jim Bowen left a mark on the young Captain. I always liked to see Jim pulling out his wad on a Sunday afternoon and some ducker missing out on a speedboat. I loved it. I was reared on epic shows like *Dallas*. Bobby and JR Ewing have got a lot to answer for.

Our back garden in Heol Glyndwr overlooked a graveyard and was a stone's throw away from The Grosvenor pub. There was a shitload of pubs in

Coedpoeth back then. It was the same with all the surrounding villages. Back then, pubs were thriving. They were the lifeblood of the community. On payday many of the workers from the steelworks in nearby Brymbo or from the local collieries would give a big wedge of their weekly wages to the landlord. And I could see why. When Mum 'n' Dad were at the pub, one of the neighbours' kids would look after us. But they'd normally have their mates come over when the coast was clear. There were no rules when the babysitter was about and I loved it.

One of the biggest events back then was the Carnival. The Coedpoeth Carnival was legendary. You were guaranteed to see a few local characters in action on Carnival Day (including my dad, Turkey). The morris dancers would be out in force, jazz bands were blowing their kazoos and there would be carnival queens and fancy-dress floats parading the streets. It was the early Eighties, not long after the rise of battles on the beaches between Mods and Rockers. Coedpoeth was definitely where the Rockers hung out. I'm no rocket scientist but as a kid, I knew their fags smelt different. Everyone came out of the woodwork for the local Carnival – it attracted characters from all the nearby villages. As a kid, I always looked forward to it. The Carnival would often end in disaster, with the natives going at it hammer and tongs in a massive punch-up, though it was difficult to work out who was fighting who. I don't think they knew either. Then there'd be sirens screeching and Black Marias arriving to halt the day's fun.

Another classic event was the Pram Race. In my mind's eye, I can still see young men with female wigs pounding down the streets in flip-flops, pushing seriously overweight, ageing babies, jammed into their prams. The race could not be run unless the contestants had downed a drink in each pub en route. It was a sight to behold – watchin' a middle-aged man dressed as Tina Turner pushing Freddie Mercury over the finishing line in a pram. In the name of charity, those characters gave it a go.

They were the good ol' days. People were up for a good crack. They didn't have much but they knew how to have a good time. It's a shame to see the demise of these iconic events.

Mum and Dad go separate ways

After years of quarrelling, the tension between Mum and Dad built up to boiling point. Being parents of two children when they were only young themselves had taken its toll. Dad left us and returned to live in Ireland, the land of his birth. I realise now that he was a likeable rogue. He and Heol Glyndwr are linked together in my memory, and Turkey is still fondly remembered by many Coedpoethians. He'd originally moved to Wrexham in his youth and ducked and dived in the construction industry. He and Mum, Kim, married when they were both just 16. They didn't split amicably – there was certainly no love lost at the time. I missed him after he left and still remember the tearful phone calls on a Saturday night.

School days

School was a kind of release from home but, as I've already said, I was an underachiever in the education department. Instead of attending a local school in Coedpoeth, I was bussed in every day to St Mary's Catholic School in Wrexham with my friend Seamus. It took me longer than others to adapt to school, and I was in a class dedicated to the slower learners. Even back then, I wasn't the coldest can in the fridge, but I soon caught up. I progressed from there to St Joseph's High School... I'll be honest – school was a shit-fest. It just didn't interest me! The highlight of my day was winding the teachers up. I used to love watching them blow. You'd often have to duck from Mr Reed's board duster. It was all one big game to me, and I was often found outside the headmaster's office.

Another highlight was the trip to and from school on the legendary G64 bus. Today's Health and Safety officers would have serious heart failure watching us dickin' about on that bus. It was like something off a *Carry On* film. Pupils bounced in the aisles and lobbed conkers out of the window as it was goin' along – just for the buzz. We'd be hangin' out the windows shouting, waving and flickin' the 'V's to random people as we whizzed past. It was funny, clockin' em lookin' back and rackin' their brains as they tried to work out who'd just shouted obscenities at them. They'd normally stand in shock for ages, just staring at the bus.

That's what most lads my age where like back then. We didn't have PlayStations or fancy tablets – we'd buzz off tormenting innocent bystanders. To us it was harmless fun, but I bet we used to annoy the duck out of some poor barstewards. Every morning the bus would take forever to get from where it picked me up to St Joseph's. It would travel more miles than Michael Palin. The bus driver must have been deaf as a post 'cos we were noisy barstewards.

While I was lucky to go to great schools, it was quite a challenge for me. At the time, I was coping with the fact that my dad was no longer living with us. I was too busy in my own world. Throughout life, I've always had a tendency to shut myself off from the real world. Fortunately, as time went on, I picked up and clawed my way into the higher sets. Quite simply, I underachieved in school because I was more interested in being Jack the Lad. At the time, that felt like more fun. I was chucked out of motor-mechanics class when I was caught sniffing the petrol from the go-kart. I tried to deny it, but I smelt like an Esso garage.

"DON'T LIE TO ME! I CAN SMELL IT ON YOUR BREATH, PHILLIPS! GET OUT!" yelled the teacher.

There was also the time I cheated on the school cross-country. If there was a shortcut, the young Captain would most definitely take it.

Taido, Nana and Olwen

I was lucky to have two sets of grandparents. Margaret and Cressville were Irish and were terrific, and really helped me after my parents' break-up. They ran a residential old people's home in Gwersyllt. I'd be there most weekends. I was the apple of Margaret and Cressville's eyes and I could never put a foot wrong with them. I was regularly found curled up on the carpet as my Taido sat in his recliner watching Dickie Davies' *World of Sport*. Deeew – he used to love the wrestling. Big Daddy and Giant Haystacks were the original dream team on a Saturday. They knew how to entertain. I loved it when Haystacks would bellow at the crowd, "I've told you before! No more Mr Nice Guy!" But ol' Haystacks always had his comeuppance against Big Daddy. It didn't matter what sport was on – Taido would watch it.

After the sport, it would be fish & chips from Arthur's Chippy. Cressville used to make his own home brew as well. Deeew, I can still smell and taste the sediment from the bottom of his glass when I think about him. Margaret, being Irish, liked her whiskey and Jesus wept, she could get it down her. She'd meet up with her friend Eryl in the launderette and they'd put the world to rights as they nailed a bottle of Bells. At the old people's home Taido and Nana ran, the residents loved me. I'd always come home with a pocketful of change. "Get yourself some sweeties from the shop, cariad!" the ol' biddies used to say to me.

Once I was that bit older and had my own bike, I'd cycle the three miles to where they lived. The first part of the cycle there was a downhill ride. It was fantastic as I was able to go faster than most cars down South Sea Hill.... If I was tired and didn't fancy the ride back up the hill to get home, I'd let down a tyre on my bike and get Cressville to drive me back in his car. Sadly that trick didn't work many times as Taido was a good handyman and would pump it up again. Taido could also cut hair – the old-fashioned bowl-cut style. Deeew, I must have looked a real tool. He was a legend: with his slicked-back grey hair and his shirt and tie – he was a cool ducker. I never once heard him raise his voice. The icing on the cake was his Robin Reliant. I loved going in it with Taido. Whenever we'd pass another Robin Reliant, they would always toot or flash as a sign of mutual three-wheeler respect. Years later I inherited the three-wheeler, though it was soon taken off me because I drove it like an idiot. But that's another story.

I also liked going to Nana Olwen's. Olwen lived in a council house in Brynteg. She had a hatch from the kitchen to the front room and used to treat me like a king. I'd be watching *Fraggle Rock* and she'd poke her head through the hatch and shout, "I'm putting the chip pan on – have some chips!"

"No, I'm OK!" I'd shout back.

"Go on, you've had nothing all day!'

"Aye, go on then, I'll have a few!" I'd reply in the end.

"What do you think this is? A bloody café?" she'd laugh back. Olwen had a heart of gold. She never had much but was very generous and would give you her last penny.

It affected me a lot when I lost my grandparents. I had some glorious moments with them. I'd do anything to spend one more Saturday with them. You don't realise how special those moments are until they've gone. Some people have never met their grandparents, never mind cherishing such special memories. I still get a few soundbites today – things like, "The biscuit barrel's full, Karl – go and help yourself... And there's some pop in the fridge too!" Deeew, I didn't half help myself. Those pink wafers went down a treat with some ice-cold lemonade. The older generation knew how to make you feel at home.

New home, but not for long

After Dad left, Mum was with someone else for a bit. We moved from Coedpoeth into Wrexham town centre. The house was in Princess Street, near the cemetery. With my sister Trina, there were four of us in the house, and I didn't like it one bit. I felt like I'd lost my identity. I'm sure I wasn't the easiest son to bring up and things were difficult between Mum and me, but I didn't get on with her new bloke. I suppose there were a couple of ways that I made things difficult for everyone. Firstly, I inevitably took my dad's side. I'd known him all my life, whereas I'd never set eyes on this other bloke who was now supposed to be a major part of things.

Also, I couldn't cope with the disruption of moving from Coedpoeth to the centre of Wrexham. I'd been familiar with the village and comfortable in it, as it was the only place I'd known. Suddenly, I was expected to accept a new father figure and a new home. It was all a bit much for me and I wasn't having any of it.

Now, knowing the other side after becoming a parent myself, I understand more about the strain of bringing up children. What a pain I must have been! Eventually the strain on Mum was too much. I had to go! I was 14, and she threw me out. One of the reasons she gave was that I spent so much time on the phone to my father in Ireland. I suppose it's much easier to appear to be a great dad when you're living hundreds of miles away and not in the same house. I have to admit, I spent a lot of time talking to him on the phone from Nana's. After all, he was my hero and I thought the world of him in those early years when he lived with us. I looked at Dad as the hero and wrongly labelled my mum as the villain.

After being thrown out, I had an embarrassing moment. My mother turned up at the office in St Joseph's School and I was summoned. There she was, holding two black bin bags full of the sum of my worldly goods. She dumped them on the floor and walked off. I was lucky not to end up in the care system. Thankfully, Uncle Paul (my dad's brother) took me in. Paul was in his mid-twenties and him and his partner Jo deserve full credit for taking in a delinquent teenager. Whilst I was no angel, I was certainly not the teenage tearaway that some might have made me out to be. Inside, all along, I was missing my father. Now Paul became the respected father figure that I needed. Under his wing, I started to gain some sort of stability.

By now I was a teenager, and my biggest issue in life was my pimply face. Deeew, I was always in Boots buying Quinoderm cream. That stuff would burn the barstewards off. I was also a regular in Superdrug. Their 49p luminous green wet-look gel was a firm favourite. There's no wonder I moult like a Labrador these days after the amounts of crap I used to put on my hair. But during the era of Kylie and Rick Astley, the young Captain had a bounce in his stride.

"Bring it on," I said. "Bring it on!"

CHAPTER TWO

Teenage Kicks

A young tearaway

So there I was: 15 years old and livin' with Uncle Paul and his partner. Living with them was good. It was nice 'cos they were both young and without all the pressures my mum had – they looked at the world through young eyes. They gave me quite a lot of freedom, allowing me to watch videos I wanted to see. They had a semi-detached house in Gwersyllt with a cellar, which they let me paint. This was the era of graffiti spray cans and breakdancing. As far as the breakdancing went, the Caterpillar was one of my signature moves. Armed with my own can of spray paint, I set about spraying the cellar with our tags.

Paul was in his twenties at the time and let's just say, he knew how to throw a party. Him and his mates used to look out for us. It was the period of paisley shirts and trousers if you were going into town on a Saturday.

When I was living with Paul and Jo, occasionally I'd wag it and skip a few lessons. The old 'dentist appointment' was one of my favourite blags at the time. This one particular day I was with five of my friends from St Joseph's. We were quite near the posh houses of Erddig. We were on our way to the country park, to skive. Ahead of us we saw a lad come out of the bushes. He had the physique of Roland Rat. He hadn't seen us so we held back a little and waited for him to duck off. We made all kinds of guesses about what the snake had been up to in the long grass: 'He hasn't gone in there for a dump!' I thought. My Spidey senses were tinglin'. We went in for a closer look, and after having a quick rummage, we found a carrier bag. We excitedly opened the bag and found it contained loads of jewellery and watches.

After a short team talk, we decided to hand it in to the cop shop. I must admit that none of us were expecting what happened. We went down the station and the copper took out a big book with different mugshots in it. We all, individually, identified the same photo. There he was – some scumbag that had been on a burglary spree. The cops' eyes lit up.

"Ladies and Gentleman – we got him!"

They had their man. But he wasn't the only ducker that was in trouble.

The cops dropped us back at school and we were about to feel the wrath of Thompson. J T Thompson.

I'd had a few run-ins with this man and tested his patience to the max. He'd only just forgiven me for the Butter Incident, when I'd taken butter from the canteen and, with the lads egging me on from afar, smeared it all over his office window. We found it hysterical.

"Yeah – have that, Thompson!" I squealed.

But, unbeknown to me, I was being watched by another teacher. My fun wasn't to last for long and I was summoned to his office.

"WHAT'S THIS, PHILLIPS?" he bellowed.

I couldn't contain myself and burst into laughter as he blew his top whilst pointing at the buttery window. I was punished and had to write more lines than Bart Simpson after that caper.

John Thompson ruled the school with an iron fist and he had no intention of calling us up onto the stage to receive the grateful applause of our fellow pupils. Deep down, I think Thompson was proud of us, as we'd given the school a good name, but we didn't get off scot-free and suffered a few days of detention.

Looking back, I tested the patience of many teachers. They deserve a lot of credit for the shit I put them through. I recently spotted my old PE teacher, Mr Mann, in B&Q. I nearly dropped dead when I saw he was in better shape than me. It's funny how I always thought they were the enemy. Now I realise that they were on our side all along.

The Maltese curfew

I had a few holidays as a teenager. My friend Matthew Aminion had grandparents in Malta and I was lucky enough to be invited to stay there for a month. His grandfather was hugely respected in Maltese society as he was a well-known doctor. As we were only about 15, we ended up being chaperoned by a priest for the flight. Jesus wept – he could talk. But little did he know, he was sat next to the Devil himself.

Matthew's grandparents lived in a nice villa. It looked over the bay and instead of buses going by the window, it was a case of yachts and ships sailing past. I'd never seen anything like it in either Wrexham or Coedpoeth. The family spent the daytime upstairs and the bedrooms were downstairs.

Matthew and I were in our final year at St Joseph's, so we had just entered the era of girls. We were on constant skirt alert. When the family had retired to bed and we were both convinced they were all asleep, we would plot our escape to victory. Everyone was expected to bed down at 9 p.m. every night. We'd both dutifully go to our bedroom and then, when we were sure it was all quiet on the sleeping front, we'd escape through the window and go down to the town. In town, we'd be like two wasps galivanting. We would creep back at 2 o'clock every morning and clamber back in through the window.

For just over a week, our nightly Great Escape worked a treat. Then Matthew sensed we were about to get caught and stopped coming out. One night soon after that, I was rumbled. On the fateful night, Matthew's grandmother brought us a drink each, only to discover that I wasn't there. I returned at about 2 a.m. and found my passage through the window blocked. 'What the?! What a disaster!' There was no way of getting through the door, either. Matthew told me that he'd had strict orders not to let me in.

As devout Catholics, needless to say, they were not too impressed and it was a case of "Forgive me, Father, for I have sinned." With just over a week of our stay left, it wasn't financially viable to fly me home early so I spent the last week under their watchful eye.

Although I'd disappointed them, they were still sound with me. But it was a different ball game from then on.

Free-time fun

As I've already mentioned, it was all about the bright-green hair gel from Superdrug, baby. Combating the cluster of zits that were making their weekly appearance was my other concern. 'OH NO, I need more Quinoderm!' Quinoderm didn't just remove the spots – it also removed the dead skin. 'Jesus wept! I'm gonna be shedding more skin than a snake by the end of the poxy week!' Lookin' my best and zit-free – that was my main ambition. Around this time, my biggest obsessions were watching *Neighbours* and *Home and Away*, Joe Bloggs jeans, dodgy Air Max and Jazz or Joop aftershave.

What could have seriously destroyed my relationship with coolness would have been my slicked-back hairdo and buck teeth. Throw in a pair of beady eyes and you're well and truly ducked. Somehow, though, I landed the lead role in the school musical of *Grease*. I got the part of Danny Zuko. As I walked onto the stage, I was asked where I'd been all summer. I replied, "I've been lugging boxes around Bargain City!"

We did that show for a whole week. Let's just say, it's a good job there were no mobile phones knocking about at the time, though there is evidence of my stint as a T-Bird on a dusty Betamax tape somewhere in Wrexham. At the time, I made the front page of the local newspaper. The headline read, 'Coolman Karl Phillips'. For once, I'd done something to make my family proud.

A lot of my teen years were spent over at my mate Ian's house in Gwersyllt. His parents often went away for long periods to their caravan in the south of France. That meant Ian and his friends – including me, of course – were, in their absence, guardians of the house and the family dog, Cuddles. Cuddles only weighed about five or six pounds. Duck knows how though, as it ate shitloads of M&S chicken. Rumour has it, I was known to enjoy some of that chicken too.

Being at Ian's house when his parents were away was like being on the set of the TV series *Men Behaving Badly*. As teenagers, we were ruled by our hormones. God knows how many hours we wasted playing computer games. Our favourite was a game called *Athlete Kings*. The only athletes in that house were the ones on the telly, 'cos we were lazy barstewards. It was a teenagers' paradise. In addition to video games, we were amazed to discover MTV: a TV channel that played our kind of music all day long.

By now, I'd left school and was doing a bit of work for Paul in his roofing business.

When Saturday came, we were ready to go for it. We'd watch *Blind Date*, then head into town to catch a few cougars. It was the rave era of the early Nineties, and up to eight of us would often pile into a van to hit the scene in Leeds or Liverpool.

The France mishap

Ian and I were like a tag team. If one of us was struggling, the other would take over and enter the ring, just like in a wrestling match. Ian's parents were really good with me, and all of Ian's friends. They invited me and another mate, Dokey, to accompany the family on a trip to the South of France. We travelled to the outskirts of Argelès in a campervan. It took us a few days. While my pockets weren't bulging back then, we had enough francs to keep the French stubbies flowing. I remember us standing around the tent like we'd conquered Everest after purchasing our first slab of pilsner.

Deeew, France become a place of many fond memories. It was a joyous moment when we encountered ladies with exposed breasts on the beach. But it wasn't so brilliant when we realised they had armpits like something out of *Gorillas in the Mist*. Everyone seemed so laid back. Their attitude to life was a lot more relaxed.

It was in France that I had a little mishap. What a disaster that turned out to be! I met and fell for this voluptuous Dutch girl. The chat and banter we shared was all leading to one outcome. 'Deeew – I'm in here! She's coming back to the tent tonight!' I thought to myself. I was like one of the lads off *The Inbetweeners*. She was a couple of years older than me and wanted a bit of the Captain. We went back to the tent just after midnight. It was beaming at 30 degrees. I was praying that it wasn't gonna be stinking in there. It didn't take us long to swing into action. Still fully clothed, we began to kiss. I then began to bump and grind. Deeew – it soon became evident that I was to run a faster race than Lynford Christie. Without notice, the map of Italy mysteriously emerged on my Wales '88 shorts. Boom! It was a case of too much, too soon for the Captain. I'll never forget the sound of the zip opening on the tent and the silhouette of the unsatisfied Dutch girl storming off in a huff, leaving the tent door flapping.

"I GO NOW... I GO NOW!!" she barked.

It was a case of *nul points* for the Welsh. As a young, beady-eyed ambassador for Wales, I'd failed miserably in building relations with our Dutch comrades.

Sadly the news of my miserable non-conquest got back across the Channel to Wrexham. My mates tormented me about the Dutch disaster for years to come.

Raving mad

It felt as though the hedonistic rave scene was hitting all the major cities. Manchester became known as Madchester, but Liverpool was our main stompin' ground. Clubs like Cream, 051 and The State were our regular haunts. I got myself into some proper messes in The State – I even managed to set my own trousers on fire one messy night. "Hey, kid – your keks are on fire!" said the Scouse lad sledging next to me. Crazy, crazy nights. On the way home, we hated going through the tunnel 'cos we'd be seeing three exits. As the designated driver, I was pulled over a few times, but I was never over the drinking limit. Back then, we were teetotal. "You look like you've had a busy night! Get yourself home to bed, lad!" said the copper, one night after I'd been breathalysed and blown zero. "You're not wrong there, Captain! Good night, officer!" I grinned.

We had some wild nights. The music we'd hummed along to in the late Seventies and early Eighties seemed tame compared to what was on offer on the house-music scene. House music ruled my world and it was all about the raves, both large and small. After a few years, Cream became the main place to go. Getting high was the norm in the rave scene. We were a part of the house-music revolution – a euphoric high that started in 1988–89 and went on and on. And boy, did my eyes bulge. Amongst all the smoke and lasers, an entire generation came up and down together. It was a loved-up vibe and we were all on the same wavelength as the doves flew high over Liverpool! You know who you are!

Jesus wept – some of those afterparties were legendary. Deeew, I'm sure half of Wrexham must have made an appearance in the back kitchen while we came crashing down to earth, with Lenny Kravitz on in the background.

Baby Bootlegger

The young Captain with Mum in the 1970s

I might LOOK like a little angel…

Me and my sister Trina rockin' the Seventies woollies

Visiting relatives in Ireland

Reading is the goal

Ex-Wales goalkeeper Dai Davies gave a talk on books and reading to school pupils at Wrexham Art Centre. The talk was part of the Clwyd Library and Museum Services programme to promote reading. With Dai are pupils of St Mary's RC School in Wrexham, from left, Karl Phillips, Malcolm Clement, Sean Jones and Ian Hooper.

I wonder what Dai Davies would make of me writing this

Forgive me Father, I'll probably sin! My First Communion

In my unofficial mid-Eighties Wrexham shirt

The pre-teen Captain showing them how it's done in the South of France

Camping trip to the South of France

With Taido in Ireland, aged 17

My Taido, Cresswell

Taido, Nan, Aunty Karen
and a young Buzz

Over in Ireland for a wedding with Buzz
and Taido

With my dad, Turkey

Footloose and fancy free in Lanzarote in the late 1990s

Early days with Claire

Ready to tunnel out of Tenko

Loadsamoney in Mexico

Rules are there to be broken!

A fine specimen of manhood

A proud dad

A bit of filming for the BBC's *Football Nation*

A crafty pint with our Ashley at the Beachcomber

A few of the Wrexham lads catching up with the Captain

A glorious piss-up in Glasgow!

A rare non-smoking photo of Geoff

A tasty weekend in Benidorm

Bootlegger 1974 Pilsner - let the carnage commence!

A vision in oils by Courtney Savage

At Bootlegger salami HQ, Cwmfarm

Away day in honour of Jacko

CHAPTER THREE

Just a
Working Man

The world of work

My teenage years weren't all about having a good time.
I left school early to take up a dead-end job in a plastics
factory. I was like Bea Smith out of *Prisoner: Cell Block H*
on a moulding machine. Jesus fuckin' wept – it was hot.
There was no one giving me roses in that gaff. They
wanted blood, for 80 quid a week. From day one, I could
never get used to that clocking in and out business. I've
always been told I'll be late for my own funeral. My every
move was being watched by an eagle-eyed screw and the
miserable décor of the place really made me regret not
listening to those who had told me to try at school.

I had to go back to St Joseph's and take my exams.
Unfortunately, I failed to cover myself in glory. And that
marked the end of a not-too-triumphant trail in the world
of education. Somehow, I'm resigned to the fact that the
teachers will never invite me back as guest speaker on
Prize-Giving Day.

I didn't last long at the plastics factory. Before I knew it, I was called into the office. In three weeks, I'd been late for eight of my shifts and had needed an early dart on a Friday to get my teeth done. I was deemed surplus to requirements.

It was great to be stuck in the house for a few weeks and not having to graft in the hellhole. But I also needed some money in my back pocket.

"You're not stayin' in bed all day, Trout. You can come with us on the roofs!"

Paul used to call me 'Trout Eyes' because I liked a smoke. To be fair, Paul made a man of me. He didn't take any nonsense. "Look at the state of you today, Trout. We can't be turnin' up to people's homes with you stinkin' like Bob Marley and askin' to use their bog for a dump all the time!" Paul ripped me good back in them days. I must have been a nightmare to have working for you. People try and rip me these days, but what they don't know is, I've been ripped from day one by the best.

Back in them days, Paul and I wouldn't leave the house until after the trolley dash on Dale Winton's *Supermarket Sweep*.

"Hey, Trout! Get some scrambled egg on the go. We'll watch this before we go and strip that roof off," Paul would go. Come to think of it, I was more of a servant than a labourer. "Get to the shop for some milk, Trout... go the chippy and get us some fish 'n' chips.... Clean the back of the van out, Trout! I want it spotless!!"

Working for Buzz taught me all about working hard and playing harder, except for a few things. I was afraid of heights and spiders – I still am. Not ideal for a roofer! I could never get out of my pit before eight o'clock. But one of the things that would most get me into trouble was the fact I couldn't even start the cement mixer. It was the old-fashioned diesel mixer that needed winding to start up. Jesus wept, even Geoff Capes would have struggled to get that barsteward goin'. And if you did manage to spark it into life, it could rip your duckin' arms off.

"For fuck sakes – you're useless, Trout. Get out of the way – this is how you do it!"

It always ended with me storming off the job. So I always made sure I had money for a bus in my back pocket. Nine times out of ten, on the way home I'd realise it was my fault.

Rowan Foods

On those occasions when the roofing jobs really got to me and I'd stormed off in a huff, I still needed to earn money, so I ended up in all kinds of places. Looking back, I had a problem keeping jobs due to my erratic ways. Back then, I got into more scrapes and escorted off more premises than Steven Seagal. In them days, you could jack a job on a Friday and start a different job on the Monday.

The majority of people my age in Wrexham would have had a stint at Rowan Foods. The place would knock out a few hundred thousand ready meals every week. Deeew – God knows how, 'cos most of the duckers that worked there were whizzed up to their eyeballs.

I was a Quality Control Operative. Imagine hiring me to quality control your luxury fish pie! They must have been desperate! I often found myself in conflict as I questioned the appearance of the shepherd's pie. I'd be at war with the love-bitten screaming banshees on the production line every time I opened my trap. In the end, I didn't even give a flying fuck! After a while I was sick of my clothes stinkin' of spag bol and fish guts. I picked up the paper one day and saw a job at a cheese factory. They give modern-day footballers grief for jumping ship for an extra 10K a week – here I was, deserting for an extra £75. It wasn't the cleverest of moves, as it involved a 45-mile round trip to Oswestry.

Jesus wept – that Audi 80 did some mileage. I bought it with a knackered gearbox and the thing drank more than Oliver Reed. By the time I'd done the maths, I would have been better off at Rowan. To add to my misery, I was on alternating 12-hour shifts, three days on, three days off (including weekends). The cheese factory was much more of a serious high-tempo place. Blocks of cheese flew at me down the production line. Fair play – some of the ladies there would work like fuck and never moan, but I was forever whingeing. "Argh, fuck – my back's killin'. My feet are in bits. What time's breaktime? I'm starving!"

Things were rosy for a few months. I worked on a line with two lovely girls called Janet and Margaret. They sort of took me under their wing and our banter would often ease the pain of the 12-hour shift. I'd serenade them with Kool & The Gang's "Let's take a walk together, near the ocean shore. Hand in hand...!" and once again they'd chime together, "You're not bloody right, lad!"

I was soon laid off, but then had a recall a few weeks later. On my return, I wasn't teamed up with Janet and Margaret – this time I was with unfamiliar faces. These ones weren't so friendly. You try working a 12-hour shift with no ducker talking to you. I felt isolated and no longer like part of a team. I was only a week into my comeback appearance when the shit hit the fan. One evening, I was asked to do a job I wasn't familiar with.

"GET ON THERE AND START PACKING THAT CHEESE!" the supervisor shouted.

"WHO THE FUCK DO YOU THINK YOU'RE TALKING TO?" I replied.

"I'M RUNNING THIS LINE!!" she barked back.

"WELL, YOU'RE NOT DOING A GOOD JOB, ARE YE?" I went. I was taken into the office.

"What's happened?" the boss asked.

"I should never have come back!" I said.

Next thing I know, I'm cleaning out my locker. I hammered it back to Wrexham in the Audi 80. 'On the bright side, at least I've got my week in hand to last me for a bit!' I thought.

Before I knew it, I was doing my scrambled egg special for Buzz again. This time around, we had Jerry Springer keeping us company. Jesus wept – it was great when things got tasty on the *Jerry Springer Show*. We'd never seen anything like this before. It was a case of working on the site, morning till night – but not until we'd seen a bit of *Jerry Springer*.

Working with Buzz sounds like heaven compared to the factories, but it wasn't all fun and games. I was in my late teens and thought the world owed me a living. I tested Buzz to the limit, and vice versa. I'd often see my arse and storm off site when he'd pushed me too far. In them days, I used to thrive on winding people up. I still do.

After another spell with Buzz, I got into the airline business. I really thought I'd made it, but if the truth be known, I was just a monkey, dipping airline parts into a toxic acid bath. One standout episode there was when I tried to wind up the resident handyman. You couldn't have met a quieter guy. I used to call him the janitor. Whenever I saw him, I'd shout in an American voice, "Heeeeeere coooomes the Janitor!" After weeks of earache off me, it got too much for this bloke.

I was in the changing rooms taking off my overalls when he walked in. I immediately jumped up and shouted, "Whooooo. It's the Janitor!" Jesus wept, he came at me like Evander Holyfield. He must have been trained by David Carradine. Before I knew it, he had me on the floor with his hands around my neck. He squeezed tightly and the life started draining out of me. The lads had to pull him off. I'd had the shock of my life and also learned a valuable lesson: not to wind people up so much. The next day, the bloke came to apologise. From that day onwards, I became more aware of my childish behaviour.

The Unfortunate Incident

When Buzz had his first kid, it didn't take me long to realise they'd have enough on their plate. Although they didn't tell me to go, I decided to look for a flat. The parents of my girlfriend at the time offered me a room in their bungalow in Gwersyllt.

Back in them days, my work would send a bus to collect their workers and take them to the factory. Jesus wept – it stank on that bus. It would pick me up by the chemist's just after 5 a.m. It was a Monday morning and I was rough as toast after a damned good weekend. On this fateful morning, I'd crept out of the house and walked up Wheatsheaf Lane to the chemist's. I was standing waiting for the bus when I had a twinge in my guts. I thought to myself, 'Oh, duck. I need to get back to the bungalow!' As I did the penguin walk back, I panicked to myself. I knew this was gonna be close. With the finishing line in sight, all hell broke loose. It was too late! 'I knew I should have had a shit!' I thought.

The second my feet touched the crazy paving leading to the bungalow, my arse exploded and it was all over the path. Each time I took a step, it left a trail.

I looked at my watch. I didn't need my Spidey senses to tell me that I wouldn't be making the bus. My biggest worry was getting to the shower without anyone seeing me. I dumped my toxic shorts in the garage. There was no way them Ocean Pacific bad boys were goin' in the bin, shit or no shit – there was at least six months left in them. Then I rinsed more than just the nutsack and got myself to work – pronto.

After the shift from hell, I got home to find the girlfriend's mam on her hands and knees, scrubbing the path. As I approached, I thought to myself, 'You've had it here, Trout. How ye gonna get out of this?!'

She looked up at me. She was seething.

"I'm gonna kill these bloody cats when I see 'em," she growled. "Look at it! It's everywhere – it's all up the path. Watch you don't tread in it, Karl!"

After tiptoeing up the path like a Russian ballerina, I made sure my first port of call was to the garage. I retrieved the Ocean Pacific shorts and got them on a boil wash – pronto.

I'm more of a dog man myself, but deeew – those cats saved my bacon that day.

Playing your carts right

I knew I'd sealed the deal for the next job when the bloke interviewing me was a mate of Buzz's. It was early spring and the council were taking on hedge and verge-cutters. For once I turned up on time, in a suit I'd got for a wedding in Ireland. Jesus wept, the thing had bigger shoulder pads than Joan Collins. To say I was overdressed was a bit of an understatement. I'm sure the bloke was buzzing off me as soon as I walked in. I went into the office and fed them the biggest amount of bullshit.

"I'm a real keen gardener. I love it mate... and I do a lot of hedge-cutting on weekends!" I waffled.

"Well," the man said, "I know you like gardening, Karl, but the only job we have left is as a road-sweeper. We think you'd be ideal for it!" he added.

I loosened my tie and undid the top button on my shirt. I took a deep breath and thought to myself, 'Eat your heart out Freddie Boswell!'

A fortnight later, I turned up for my first day in the new job and was issued with a yellow cart, a broom, a shovel and a shitload of binbags. I was also given a set of grey overalls. Fuckin' 'ell – I looked like Michael Myers, stompin' up and down Rhos High Street. They made me wear a big honkin' pair of boots. Deeew – by lunchtime, I felt like I'd walked to Zimbabwe and back. I won't lie: on the first day or two, I felt embarrassed as I mooched about. But after a few days, I'd get some nice feedback on my rounds – "Deeew – you're doing a bloody good job there, lad!"

Traipsin' around the streets with that friggin' cart, sweepin' up chip wrappers and sweating my nutsack off, was hard work. 'Duck dis shot. I'll do it in my Audi!' I thought. There was no more walking more miles than The Proclaimers back to the lock-up.

The lock-up was an absolute dump – an old garage. It wasn't the type of place you could go for a skive or a crafty forty winks, 'cos it hummed in there. There were no windows and no ventilation. This was where I was supposed to eat my lunch and take a break.

Doing the rounds in the Audi seemed like an amazing brainwave. It gave me more time to top up my tan in the summer sun. Once again, I thought I was big and clever. But my shirking shenanigans weren't going to last forever. I think I took things a bit too far when I started playing golf on the local 9-hole course during my shift. I felt like Seve Ballasteros.

Seeing me teeing off in them big boots and boiler suit must have been some sight. Then one fateful afternoon, I returned to the lock-up and the gaffer was there. I parked the Audi around the corner.

"Where you been, Karl?" he asked.

"Just been around the powerhouse!" I said.

"I'll be honest with you, mate: you've been seen clacking golf balls in Pen Y Cae and basking in the sun on the rugby pitch when you're meant to be on your rounds. We're gonna need to let you go!" he said.

He knew and I knew that I'd been taking the piss... so that was the end of that job.

At this time, I was in the process of trying to get my own place... and because I'd worked for the council, they found me a one-bedroom flat in Gwersyllt. It was in what I call Gwersyllt's Bermuda Triangle – once you move in there, you never leave. The flat was in a great spot on the first floor. I could stare out of the window and see every ducker coming and going.

Tŷ Capal

Living at Tŷ Capal was the start of an exciting era. I went to town on the flat and did all the kitchen units with Stain and Grain. "Deeew – this has come up good, Doug!" I said to myself. I even got the obligatory dado rail up in the hallway. It was classic Nineties décor with the cheapest laminate out of China.

Living on my own came with responsibilities. Bills needed paying. My problem was, I wasn't facing the responsibility of paying them. I was getting into a vicious cycle of never-ending debt. Around this time, I started ordering tidy clothes from the catalogue, while never making the payments. The intercom was always buzzing: "Another delivery for Eddie Phillips!" I was selling the clothes and trainers to the lads down the pub. This was something that was going to come back to bite me on the ring-piece at a later date.

Meanwhile, my work record was shockin'. I'd get a job and then, after a bit, I'd be back with Buzz. "Back again, Trout!" he'd shout. "I don't want any of your crap this time. I'm the boss here!"

One thing was for sure – there was plenty of work back then. But if I could choose between working in a factory and working with Buzz, it would be with Buzz. With Buzz, it wasn't as regimented.

When I look back at how easily I flitted from one job to the next, I realise that I was very lucky. Come to think of it – I owe you a drink, Buzz!

CHAPTER FOUR

A Few Light Ales

Hello, alcohol!

To date, at the time of going to print, I've been drinking for nearly 30 years. When you're in your twenties, you think you're The Man and can get away with everything. At that tenacious age, I'd go into town at weekends with the lads, looking for cougars. They were great nights, often made even better by the fact we normally managed a few cans before heading for the nightspots. By then, as well as the rave scene of other cities, we were old enough to savour the delights of local pubs.

The Wheatsheaf in Gwersyllt has been my local since day one. Back then, it was run by Tony. When he took it over, it had a reputation as a fairly rum, even dangerous, place and he wanted to build it up again. He was firm but fair. It was a regular occurrence to see people being thrown out, sometimes literally. A few days later there'd be a knock on his door and, as long as they apologised, they were back in. He was old school. Fair play to him: I had to knock his back door and apologise a few times. The good thing about him was he never held a grudge.

Back then, pubs were full of characters. Like Tony Bell, who smoked his fags hardcore. He'd rip off the filter then light up, with the words, "Get that inside you, boy." And his mate 'John Bad Rock', who worked at the local slaughterhouse and had hands larger than shovels. John Bad Rock and Tony would sit around and swear more than Roy Chubby Brown. They used to take the piss out of us young lads. They'd regularly growl at us, but I'm sure they liked us deep down. Deeew – there were some good hard-drinking characters in the boozer back then. There still are in the Wheat. They don't give a flying duck who you are. You could burst into flames and no ducker would turn around.

One night, after a few ales, I got myself into a bit of bother. I was in my early twenties. It was just before midnight and me 'n' my mate were the last to leave. It took the landlord ages to get rid of us. He slammed the door the second we walked through it. Just as I left the pub, the fresh air hit me and I was gagging for a slash. But the bolt was on, so I couldn't go back in. I found myself slashing all over the wall outside.

Bliss. Well, it was at first. In mid-flow, I became aware of a flashing blue light. The rozzers came out of nowhere. A copper approached me and asked me to stop. I was away with the fairies – there was no stopping me.

"PUT IT AWAY!!" he commanded.

"This ain't stoppin', baby," I replied. He then proceeded to leather me with his truncheon. He waded into my legs.

He went on to say on record that he only struck me once. Jesus wept – that ducker gave me a friggin' limp!

I drunkenly resisted arrest and found myself banged up in the county jail. After a night in the cells, I was up at the crack of dawn. Then I realised that during the struggle to get me in the car, I must have shit myself. I woke up with the hangover from hell and I was reeking! The slit in the door opened. It was an old schoolfriend that had just come on shift.

"I knew it was you. You OK, lad?" he asked.

"Oh – Jesus! I shit myself!" I replied. Fair play, he sorted me out with a shower and a grey Fruit of the Loom tracksuit.

A few days later, I was in court. Buzz turned up for some moral support. I stood up in the docks, wearing my Lacoste jacket, with my hands in my pockets.

"STAND UP STRAIGHT AND GET YOUR HANDS OUT OF YOUR POCKETS!" screamed the judge.

That episode made me take a good look at myself. "Not so cocky now, are you, Trout? You need to sort your shit out!" Buzz barked when we got back to the van. I was determined never to get into bother as bad as that again.

They say lightning doesn't strike twice, but Jesus wept – it struck me again! Not long after the first incident, I was apprehended again for slashing on a public road. Once again, the demon drink had clouded my judgment.

This time my drunken antics were caught on CCTV. The CCTV operator had followed me running down the High

Street and up an alleyway. By the time the cops arrived, I was in full flow. This time, thankfully, it was an on-the-spot fine. I was convinced this would be my last brush with the law. Every time I was going out, it was costing me a week's friggin' wages.

It's fair to say that the Nineties were naughty. But we were just young lads having a good time and hurting nobody, bar ourselves.

Drunk in Jamaica

I had a close scrape after a few ales in Jamaica while on holiday there with a mate. I'd had my heart set on seeing the ganja plantations. Obviously, there were no official trips to the ganja fields. We were warned not to go into the hills. But we got talking to a bloke in the hotel lobby who said he'd take us to meet his mate, 'up in the hills'.

"You keep this quiet, mon. You walk out the gates and wait outside, in the morning. I'll be waiting for you. I'll show you the real Jamaica!"

The following morning, the driver was there. Now, I've driven some heaps of shit in my life, but this ducker's motor looked shot.

"He's definitely got no MOT on this ducker, Daz!" I said.

"Looks like he's had a few bumps! Look at the back end," Daz replied.

The back bumper looked like he'd been rammed by Bob Marley's tour bus. Me 'n' Daz got in.

"What's your name, mate?" I asked.

"You call me Bossman!" he replied. "You like reggae?" he asked, as he floored it towards the hills. From the back seat, I studied him. You couldn't work out how old he was. When we asked him, he laughed and replied, "I'm nearly as old as this car, mon. She's alright!"

Not long into the journey, Bossman asked, "You wanna stop for a drink, mon?" So we stopped at a roadside bar. We ordered a few Red Stripes and Bossman said he wanted a rum. We were more than happy to buy him a rum, but this ducker had a glassful of Appleton's finest.

"You 'avin another Red Stripe for the road, boys?" he asked after a few gulps. Before we know it, his lips are around another glass of rum.

"Fuckin' 'ell! He can get it down him, Trout!" Daz says to me on the quiet. We were happy to stop for a drink, but we didn't realise that Bossman was such a fan of the top shelf. His eyes were glazed over and judging by the smell of his smoke, he was most definitely chilled out.

"Good for the soul, mon!" he laughed with the barman. He laughed like the voodoo man off *Live and Let Die*. "You boys relax now. Bossman gonna show you a real good time! The real Jamaica!" he cackled. We got the feeling that Bossman was more than just a regular in this establishment.

A song came on the radio. "Turn it up, mon!" Bossman shouted at the barman. Jesus wept – it wasn't even 12 o'clock and Bossman was dancin' on the side of the road.

"Deeew – you wouldn't have got this if you'd booked through Reception!" I said to Daz.

"I'm hungry now. You want some jerk chicken?!" Bossman asked.

"We had a few poached eggs before we left... But it's your day as well as ours. So let's check it out!" I said.

He then drove us to a barbecue place up the road. The rum must have hit him hard 'cos he didn't take the motor out of second gear. By now, me and Daz were wondering if we should have taken the advice of the travel rep. The barbeque was under a corrugated tin roof. It was lunchtime and the place was swarming. While me 'n' Daz didn't have much appetite for the chicken, we were more than happy to get another round of drinks in... and indeed a chicken platter for Bossman. While at the bar, we were approached by a guy that scared the living shit out of me. I turned to my side and he appeared from nowhere.

"You want black 'ash?" he asked. I'm not one for profiling, but let's just say his presence was unnerving.

"Black Ash?" I asked.

"No – HASH... real Jamaican Gold... We call it gum, mon!!" he replied. He opened his withered hand and showed a big ball of black hash. "You can take it... for $250!" he said.

"Aye, mate. I haven't got $250 in the hotel, never mind in my back pocket!" I replied. What little money we did have on us, Bossman was already making a big dint into it. Deeew – anybody would have sworn it was

Bossman on his holiday, not us. In the meantime, this man was going on about the black hash. Jesus wept – he wouldn't leave us alone. So we supped up and left.

We were soon back on the road, churning into the hills. Bossman's car made light work of the steep inclines. About 40 minutes later, we came into a big village, which seemed to be perched high in the sky. The scenery was breathtaking. Huge green mountains, covered in trees.

"Here we are!" he said, triumphantly. Bossman explained that it wasn't possible to take us to the huge plantations as they were run by gangs, but that he'd take us to see his Rastaman friend, who had a load of it growing. "He has a beautiful garden!" Bossman said.

Bossman wasn't lying – Rastaman did indeed have a load of it. His back garden was full of plants that had not long started flowering. Mmmmm – the air was full of the sweet smell of natural goodness. He was growing all sorts of fruit and veg in his yard.

'Deeew – you don't see these sorts of characters on *Gardeners World*!' I thought.

Rastaman had a nice warm aura about him and made us feel comfortable. He was the polar opposite of the Black Hash man. He gave us a guided tour of his garden, though we couldn't understand what he was saying. It sounded like he was rambling in Jamaican Klingon. But deeew, we were on the same wavelength. We slipped him a few bob... and let's just say we didn't come away empty-handed. We then had a few smokes with Bossman and Rastaman. It soon became evident that they could smoke a lot more than us.

After a few more smokes, Bossman informed us that he was thirsty again. So we got back into the car, and Bossman drove to a bar. The bar was situated on a crossroads. There were only three people in there when we rocked up, but as soon as we parked our arses on the barstools, it seemed like the whole village turned up. Bossman was soon up to his old tricks – gulping the rum and putting it on our tab. So was half the bar.

"Duckin' hellfire. We're gonna end up giving away more money than Bob Geldof, Doug!" I said to Daz.

I settled up with the barman and then announced that we were leaving. By now, Bossman had well and truly rinsed us.

"No," said a stocky little man in a white vest. "You leave a li'l deposit for me, mon!" he demanded.

"Deposit? I can't even pay my rent, never mind a deposit!" I said. Bossman stepped in and exchanged what sounded like terse words.

"GET IN THE CAR, BOSS!!" Bossman screamed. Daz and I did just that. We both darted into the back of the car and tried to lock the doors. But the doors wouldn't lock. The windows didn't even go up. There was no rushing Bossman, though. He walked back to the car like he had all day.

"Deposit!!! These people not my friends!" Bossman exclaimed on our journey back.

How I didn't shit myself in the back of his car is a miracle. It was a good job I passed on the jerk chicken 'cos I would've definitely filled my pants that day. Bossman steered us safely back to our base and dropped us off at the gates of our hotel. Deeeew – that trip with Bossman was certainly an interesting one. From the state of us, I'm sure every ducker in that hotel must have known we'd been on a 'sightseeing tour' with Bossman. We were more than glad to get back to our room and sample some of our merchandise that evening.

Taking a pasting

I've never been one for the active type of holiday, but I joined the lads on a ski-trip to Andorra one year. What an absolute friggin' disaster that turned out to be.

Andorra was known as a good haunt for those who wanted a bit of action off the slopes as well as on it. There was a good mix of lads going: those who couldn't wait to go skiing and those who wanted to get rat-arsed. I was a nervous wreck on the slopes. With my fear of heights, just getting on one of those chairlifts scared the living crap out of me. I couldn't get over the fact that people enjoyed this shit.

But make no bones about it, the Captain soon got into the swing of it – thanks to some expert tuition from one of my pals, Len. Fair play, Len took a lot of time out to show some of the lads how it was done.

Whilst I enjoyed the scenery, skiing was most definitely not for me. After a few days, my body was aching like fuck. A few of us had had enough of the skiing lark by now. So we gave it a miss and spent the rest of the holiday getting on it.

The last day turned out to be a grueller. We got up for breakfast and Lenny was on it straight away. Somehow, he'd got hold of a pellet gun and was making a proper nuisance of himself. There he was, in his vest, taking pot-shots at random strangers. It all started off like a bit of banter, but by evening the mood definitely took a turn for the worse.

I was beered out, so I got on the Malibu. Meanwhile, he was still at it. Nearing the end of the night, after a lot of jumping up and down to Cypress Hill, I made my way back to the room. As I approached the stairs, a few of the lads that had been in the bar earlier tried to soak me with a large bucket of water. Deeew – the barstewards got me good style. Thing is, after several hours on the Malibu, I didn't find it funny. I saw red. I've never been one for using my fists, mainly because I'm no good with them, but the soaking was like a red rag to a bull. I charged towards them and launched a big wild haymaker.

"C'mon, you fuckers!" I screamed. I missed by a country mile and slipped on the wet tiles and tumbled to the floor. I was then kicked from one end of the corridor to the other. All hell broke loose and there was now a running pitched battle. Back-up arrived and we proceeded to have a drunken row in the corridor. After the fracas quietened down, we found one of our lads hiding under the bed. He never lived that down. Soon the police were on the scene. Our passports were handed over and we were warned that we wouldn't be returning home if there were any more antics.

Deeew – I woke up with the hangover from hell. All I could smell and taste was poxy coconut. I was rough as duck. To this day, I won't go near that stuff. Obviously, it wasn't the Malibu that was the real problem, it was the daft ducker drinking it. I'll never forget hobbling around Toulouse Airport in agony. Every time I took a breath, I felt a shooting pain in my ribcage – a painful reminder of the size 9 that had given me a good seeing to the night before.

I can remember only one other incident that bore any resemblance to the Andorra beating. That happened when I was ten. Walking alone to my Nana's house in Brynteg on the outskirts of Wrexham, I got followed by a group of other lads. So I made a dart for it. They came after me. Initially I made good ground on them and turned round and flicked the 'V's at them.

"C'mon, you wankers!" I shouted.

But just like life, it was a marathon and not a sprint. My stamina deteriorated after dashing up Moss Valley Hill. Before I knew it, they'd closed the gap. I knew there was no way I was gonna make it to Nana's. They surrounded me like a pack of wild hyenas – there was no escaping

this one. For some daft reason, I decided to blag the ol'
Karate Kid move in the hope it would scare them off. I
perched on one leg and lifted both arms in the air and
arched them like Danny LaRusso. I was hoping those
duckers were gonna think I knew a bit of karate. Sadly,
they didn't give two flying ducks about karate. They
came in for the kill. It didn't take them long to get me
on the floor, and then they proceeded to boot the living
daylights out of me. The fact that one of the barstewards
was wearing wellies made me feel even more sorry for
myself – I couldn't even outrun that ducker. I could run a
bit, but I was definitely no Seb Coe. I was more of a 100-
metre hurdles type of guy. Deeew – I didn't half spy my
arse and regretted flicking the 'V's at them every time I
received a boot to the body. But I was a cheeky ducker
back then. It was a harsh lesson. My whole body looked
like a rotten piece of fruit after that unfortunate incident.

CHAPTER 5

Travellers' Tales

The Boudoir

OK, so by now it's about 1999 and I'm living the bachelor life after splitting up from my previous girlfriend. I nicknamed my flat The Boudoir and it was a hive of activity amongst the lads, especially if there was a big footy match on. European Football Nights on Wednesdays were legendary. I'd regularly be cooking a big joint of beef or a nice piece of cheap pork for the boys. Or we'd be over the road at the Wheatsheaf, having a right good midweek go at it.

At this point, I need to let you know – the Boudoir was far from being a palace. I didn't have a washing machine or even curtains. But it was my castle and I was proud of it. There was a masculine musk to the Boudoir which would linger, with the tobacco smell battling the waft of cheap deodorant.

There was a couple of old ladies living in the same block. One smoked more than my Audi 80 and the other never missed a trick. But they were good neighbours. I also had a pal living below me called 'Shaun Skunk'.

Shaun was a big lad and to call him a loose cannon would be an understatement. His tasty smokes were of the exotic kind. Smoke would drift out of his window to the tune of 'Naaaaa Naaaaa Naaaa na-na-na' as he immersed himself in another episode of *Coronation Street*. He was a rum lad, but he had a soft spot in his heart for the soaps.

We all looked out for each other. Living in the flats, our mixed motley crew may have been the downtrodden, but having the independence made up for being skint. Deeew – I was forever pressing the emergency button on the electric meter back then.

It was about this time that I met Claire, after a drunken night down the Wheatsheaf. From the first time we met, we got on really well. Little did I know that those first few dates would lead to the beginning of a new life. Back in them days, Claire and I would have some epic drinking sessions. But, like all couples, we had our fair share of blazing rows too. Looking back, I think what helped was that she had her own group of friends, so I was still able to live the life of Riley while goin' out with my mates. She wasn't on my case, so I didn't feel under pressure to change my erratic ways. However, there were a couple of rude awakenings on the horizon.

First things first, I had a two-week stint in Ibiza with the lads booked. Jesus wept! How the duck did we do two weeks in Ibiza? It was a riotous fortnight, to say the least. My budget was low and a fair share of it was blown on Senegalese sunglasses. But where there's a will, there's always a way and it's fair to say that we were blasted every night of that holiday, baby. Amongst other things, there was smoking with the Moroccans and late-night drinking at the Pussycat Bar in the San Antonio Bay area. This was one of our many legendary trips to the White Isle. Over the years, we've had some bangin' times out there. Me 'n' the lads definitely left a mark on the place.

Talk about 'Murder on the Dancefloor' – I had one mate shit his pants on it! There we were, bobbing up and down on the spot in Es Paradis, surrounded by beautiful people and nearing the heights of euphoria, when there was the sudden unmistakable waft of shit in the air! People were passing and you could hear, "It stinks – ughhhh!"

After a bit of detective work, it wasn't hard to nail the suspect. I looked at him and asked, "Aye, have you shit yourself? It fuckin' honks, mate!!"

He was in no fit state to answer me back. He looked at me sheepishly and nodded slowly. It was most definitely time to leave the scene of the crime, baby. No shame – as ambassadors of the Wreck-Head Society, I'm sure he wasn't the first and or the last to shit himself on the dancefloor. We had a right laugh watching him, spangled, trying to have a shower. And an even better one trying to dispose of his rancid jeans in a bin over the road. It was a refreshing change to witness someone else coming home stinking of shit, and not me.

I won't deny it, I got in some terrible messes out there myself. But that's what Ibiza is all about. It's a coming-of-age place. Many a time I've been at the airport, waiting for my late-night return flight, saying to myself, "I'm never coming back again" – only to book another trip a few weeks later.

On my return from this fortnight, I was a broken man. Coming back into Wrexham, I was skint and knackered. I got back to the Boudoir and it was unrecognisable. Claire had painted the place, put curtains up and bought cutlery for the drawers. There was also grub in the fridge. 'This doesn't smell like my flat!' I thought, as I walked in. 'Hang on. This doesn't even look like my flat!' There and then, I knew I had a keeper.

When it hits the fan

Remember I told you about the time when I was ordering swag from the catalogue under the name Eddie Phillips? Well, it was only a matter of time until that all caught up with me. I'm now a big believer in the old saying, 'You reap what you sow.' It all hit the fan when I had an unexpected visit from Mr Bryan Edwards, AKA Wrexham's answer to Paul Bohill from *Can't Pay? We'll Take It Away!* I'd just got home after an early dart. The barsteward must have clocked me going into my Boudoir because the next thing I knew, there was a knock on the door. I didn't even have a chance to put the poxy kettle on – he must have gained access by snaking in before the front door shut. He knocked on the door to my flat a few times and then flapped the letterbox. I refused to answer. Fair play, this persistent ducker wasn't going away. Here I am, in the hallway of my flat, pinned to the wall like Spiderman, trying to be Mr Invisible. I was too scared to move in case he heard my feet shuffling on the cheap 100% non-recyclable laminate.

'For duck's sakes!' I thought. After living it large in Ibiza for two weeks, I was on the bones of my arse. There was no way I had money to sort this ducker out after drinking cocktails through a straw out of a glass boot for the last fortnight.

I peeped towards the door, at the letter box. He'd lifted the flap and I could see his lips through the metal frame. "Come out, Karl. I know you're in there!" he shouted. I just stuck to the wall. My Spidey senses didn't need to tingle for me to know that I was well and truly ducked! "Have it your way then, Karl!" he warned. "There's a van outside with roofing batons on. I could have a word with a few people regarding your working status!" I could hear him walking away. Just then, I had a flood of conscience and decided to face the music.

"Opening that door was the best move you've ever made!" he said.

I was always a fool in my younger days. My biggest problem was not addressing things. I'd ignore letters and not answer phone calls. Another example was when I passed my driving test. I had two friggin' years to fill in my pass certificate and send it off for a licence. But because I was too slow and lazy to get round to it, I had to retake the test. So when people ask me if I passed my driving test first time, I always answer, "Well... technically – yes. But un-technically – 'NO', baby!"

Another one from the Boudoir days was when I got rumbled off the TV licence man. I was sat in the Boudoir with my mate Dali. To say Dali was loud would be an understatement. He was one of those lads that couldn't be quiet if his life depended on it. We were chilling out, watching the footy and swilling a few of Lidl's finest when there was a knock on the door. I was normally suspicious if this happened, because nine times out of ten, it was a ducker trying to 'catch up with me' about something.

This time I opened the door as we were expecting another one of the lads, but lo and behold – it was the poxy TV licence man. The weasel stood there with a high-vis draped over his skinny frame, reeking of fags. I'd never seen fingers singed like that before.

"Mr Phillips. We meet at last! I have reason to believe you have a television in use in your property. In fact – I can hear one!"

The telly was on full blast. All you could hear was Tony Gubba describing the growing pressure from the away side. 'You're not wrong there!' I thought to myself.

"I need to gain access to your property!" demanded the weasel.

I've never been the coldest can in the fridge, but I knew I wasn't getting away with this one. Having said that, there was no way I was letting Weasel Man in. "Right – I'm going to report you to the courts!" he announced.

A few weeks later, there I was: facing Wrexham's magistrates for another minor misdemeanour. Straight after the court appearance, I nipped over to the fines office to arrange payment.

I explained to the clerk that I'd just been fined for non-payment of TV licence. To my surprise, I received a standing ovation from the others awaiting their penance! What with the catalogue and the TV licence fine, it was gonna be a tight few months. It was an expensive lesson, but we all need to face up to responsibility (sooner, rather than later).

Ring sting in Goa

After the dealings with the repo man and the TV licence man, it took me a few months to get back on my feet again. It was a matter of laying low for the foreseeable future. Having Claire around helped me put everything in perspective and just take one day at a time. As well as the burden of having to pay the different fines, I'd get a regular ripping off Buzz too – something along the lines of, "Still paying those fines off, Trout? Thought you were being clever, didn't ye?! Hopefully this new woman of yours has got you on the straight 'n' narrow!"

Credit where it's due – Claire was a stabilising influence. So when it came up to holiday time, it would have been wrong of me to go on another lads' jaunt. It was time to take Claire on an adventure. Two tickets to Goa, please!

Everyone who goes to Goa from Britain seems to come back gushing about the place. It's a beautiful region of India, bordering the Arabian Sea. We went just after Christmas. Around about that time of year, work was always a bit slack and the weather was bleak, so it was a perfect destination to escape the winter blues.

Claire's mum and dad had been the year before and wouldn't stop raving about the place. They couldn't get over how cheap it was.

"Deeeww – I'll have a bit of that!" I said to myself.

Over the next few weeks, I trawled the internet for a deal. I soon found it: a tidy two-week bed and breakfast in Candolim, the resort where Claire's parents had been.

"That'll do me – pack your bags, we're off!!" I went.

I was buzzin'. This was the furthest I'd ever been. We were both looking forward to experiencing a different type of holiday. The first noticeable difference was the length of the friggin' flight. There we were, packed in like duckin' sardines. A few hours into the flight, we were served drinks and a light bite.

And then the awkward barsteward in front of me decided to recline her seat – all the way back. It turned out her and her mate had popped a couple of sleeping tablets. So there she was, snoring like a walrus – and my legs were trapped.

"We should've booked those extra-legroom seats. I can't sit like this for another poxy six hours!" I complained to Claire.

After the flight from hell, I felt like death warmed up. So we didn't get the transfer bus: we grabbed a taxi. Just my luck – the one we took fancied himself as Michael Schumacher. Deeeww – I'd never seen a Rascal van go so quick. Don't get me wrong, I was in a rush to get to the hotel, but not as much of a rush as this ducker. We got to the hotel at 5 a.m. We were excited – it was too late to go to bed, so we waited until sunrise. To say our first walk into town was an eye-opener was an understatement. We passed a restaurant called Fisherman's Cove and got a waft of what smelt like fermented fish guts.

"What the fuck have we come here for?!" I exclaimed to Claire.

"You booked it!" she replied.

It was a total culture shock and I started to think that I'd made a massive mistake. On our short route to the beach we passed packs of wild dogs, barking like fuck at the state of the pale Welshman as he walked by in his flip-flops. You needed eyes in the back of your head. The motorbikes scared the shit out of me as they whizzed passed and beeped their horns. I was a nervous wreck. And then I had to contend with the street hawkers, who wanted to flog me a suitcase full of T-shirts. We made our way to a shack called Wagamama. Claire's mum had recommended the place, mainly because it had a 'British toilet'. Jesus wept – I was soon to be a regular at this particular toilet.

It was early morning and there wasn't a cloud in the sky. I parked my arse on a sun lounger and ordered an egg and chips. Here I was, on a beach in India and ordering egg and chips. That was, without a doubt, one of the best egg and chips I'd ever had, though. They even served it with a nice bit of bread and butter.

I soon felt the fatigue of the flight and fell asleep. Claire woke me up after a few hours. Jesus wept – it was beaming. My eyes were like slits. I needed to get back to the room. I spent the rest of the day sleeping under the air-conditioning unit as Claire unpacked.

By early evening, I could smell something burning. "Smells like someone's got a bonfire on the go," I said to Claire. They were burning rubbish out there. Deeeww – no doubt about it, they did things differently here. I just needed to get used to a few things.

I wasn't brave enough to sample the local cuisine yet, so we headed to a gaff called Tony's Place for fish, chips and mushy peas. Deeeww – I was well and truly flying the flag of a Welshman abroad. Eat your heart out, Rick Stein – this was a damned good fish and chips. To be honest, I'm ashamed to admit, I spent most of the time moaning to Claire. But a few days in, I was getting used to their way of life. Slowly but surely, I started to feel at ease.

On the fourth night I had a bit of a revelation. We were at a beach bar, listening to a bit of Goan trance. I sat and watched the waves coming in as the sun disappeared below the horizon. The sky was turned a Martian red. A shiver ran down my spine. I felt like I'd been kissed by Lord Shiva. The Goan trance resonated in me and I felt nothing but love.

"Deeeww – I'm starting to like this place!" I said.

"I know. And we haven't spent a hundred quid yet!" Claire replied.

The following day, I was up with the lark and began to feel more comfortable. I decided to book a few daytrips and do a bit of sightseeing. Old Goa is renowned for old churches, but I didn't get around to visiting any as I was more interested in watching the sun go down.

Getting to know you

While lying on the beach and soaking up the sun, I enjoyed killing a bit of time with the local beach hawkers, who were parading up and down, trying to flog their various wares. I bought them all for a bit of friggin' peace: magnetic chessboards, magic mushroom T-shirts, Rajasthani bongo drums, lotus beads, fake replica cricket tops and strawberries – I don't even like friggin' strawberries! Come to think of it, I'm duckin' shot at chess, too. I did enjoy the banter, though. I used to buzz off the whole interaction with those characters out there. Jesus wept – they had me hook, line and sinker!! You had to admire them – they were proper grafters.

By now, I was opting for the local dishes. I tried the spicy calamari in vindaloo sauce. I mopped it up with the tastiest garlic-cheesy naan. Deeeww – I was well and truly loving it.

"That's gonna make you bad. You know what you're like with spicy food!" Claire warned me.

"Don't be daft, woman!" I replied.

The portion was small and I liked it that much, I told 'Chef El Vino' to get another plateful on the go.

"You won't be going far tomorrow!" Claire said.

"You watch me!" I replied.

The next day, we were on the beach. Mid-afternoon, we made our way back to the room, taking a shortcut through an alley. This would soon be christened 'Shit-Pant Alley'. I'm not proud of this incident, but it was a day of reckoning. The previous night's spicy calamari was brewing. As I shuffled along in my flip-flops, I said to Claire, "I need the bog – NOW!"

"I told you this would happen!" she said.

I jumped over a wall, but as I did, I must have hit reverse and I knew the clutch had gone. I shit myself. It was like I'd opened a tap and was filling a bath.

'I shouldn't have had that second portion of spicy calamari!' I thought.

I ditched my shorts, jumped back over the wall and got a towel round me. I made a mad dash for it back to the hotel for a shower.

The following day, we walked back to our room via the same shortcut. There in the alley, I saw my shorts. Unbeknown to me, I'd jumped into some ducker's garden, and the owner of the garden must have lobbed them back onto the path. Each day as we came past, the shorts were further along the alleyway. Jesus wept – they nearly made it onto the main stretch. People must have been having a damned good rummage in the hope of finding some swag. Deeeww – they must have had a nasty surprise when they realised that them Ocean Pacific shorts had the Captain's Log in them! The Captain's rear-end was well and truly shot in Goa. After that explosion, I had an arse like a baboon and needed to be within a safe distance of a British toilet at all times.

That holiday taught me that you don't need to be surrounded by modern-day luxuries like you are in Europe. By the end of that trip, I was unfazed by the smell of burning rubbish or growling packs of dogs. I liked the place and the nice people. I've gone on to lose a few brain cells dancing under those Goan coconut trees.

Our first home

It must have been about 2003. I was working on the roofs after being escorted off the premises of two cheese factories. This was after a couple of irregularities regarding my conduct. Claire and I had been together about three years and we'd been saving for over a year. To tell you the truth, Claire was a better saver – I was a bit of a weekend millionaire. A council house came on the market just up the road from the Boudoir, on First Avenue. The second I saw it, I rushed to the estate agent's. I walked in and said, "That house on First Avenue that's just gone up for sale – I'll have it!"

I hadn't even asked Claire. I knew there was potential in this house as a friend of mine (Rawly) owned one over the road. The estate agent looked at me funny. "Don't you want to see it first?"

Like a dick, I offered them an extra grand to take it off the market. An old couple had passed away and left it to their family, who wanted to sell it. It was a quick sale. I wasn't interested in the ins and outs – I just wanted it. Before we got the keys, I had it all planned. I was going to gut it to bare brick and whack an extension on the back of it. Oh yeah, baby – a nice open-plan back kitchen. Duck knows how I was going to pay for it, but my mates from the Wheatsheaf were in the building game and were willing to help me out.

Once we collected the keys, I excitedly took my mate Liam, who was a plumber, to see it. After showing him around, he congratulated me and agreed the place had a lot of potential.

"Fair play, Trout. Not a bad gaff, this. Where's the gas come in?" he asked.

I took him into the back kitchen and showed him the pipes coming in. He pulled the pipes and they came out of the wall.

"This isn't right. What the f*ck's goin' on here? This place hasn't got any gas, Trout. This is gonna cost you!"

The dirty stinking barstewards. The sneaky duckers had put in a dummy gas connection to make it appear like they had gas.

It did indeed cost me/us. Claire still goes on about it. It cost us about three grand to put that right – three grand we didn't duckin' have. It took a while and a lot of favours, but after a lot of sweat, tears and cheap cans of lager, we got it done. I christened it Café Avenue. I signed up in DFS for two new leather settees on the knock. One minute I was admiring them in the showroom, the next minute I was sat on one of them, drinking cheap champagne after signing on the dotted line. Because we were spending a fortune on the house, I'd find myself asking Buzz for a sub.

"F*ckin' hell, Trout. You need to stay out of that Wheatsheaf. I haven't got a big settee like you. And you've got two of the bastards!"

He was right. But those settees were comfy, even if they did take five years to pay off. We had many a good time at Café Avenue. It was a tidy upgrade from the Boudoir. But times were tough – it wasn't on a plate. All the things that I'd acquired on the knock needed paying for. Buying things on the never-never meant keeping things tight, which meant going out less and dining in and entertaining more. It was about now that I started enjoying cooking and honing my culinary skills. I was a big fan of Keith Floyd and would often try and replicate some of his recipes, while swilling some of Lidl's finest. Claire would often film me acting the goat in the back kitchen. Keith Floyd would've been proud of my slow-roast lamb recipe. I'd bang it in the oven and then take it out nine pints later. Mmmmm – melt in your mouth, baby!

Café Avenue had the ultimate back kitchen where one could eat, drink and be merry.... and that's an understatement. Claire and I have got some fond memories of that place, with some legendary Christmas dinner parties. We lived there for 14 years.

Shit happens

After eventually getting the house sorted and managing to just about keep our heads above water, we rewarded ourselves with a break. To be honest, we were borrowing off one credit card to pay the other.

Claire and I love Benidorm. Don't get me wrong, it's nice to visit far-flung exotic locations, but sometimes it's good to keep it simple. This putrid tale happened a bit more recently, when we were with our son, Iwan, in a place called Calpe, just north of Benidorm.

On this particular day we were at a nice restaurant with Iwan nestled in his pushchair. The waitress was particularly helpful and pleasant, and attractive. She took a real shine to Iwan and made many suggestions about what dishes to try. After a few "Dos cervezas por favor!",

I was beginning to think, 'Your wish is my command.' Boy, she got me hook, line and sinker with her descriptions of the food. We had a cracking afternoon in that bar, eating, drinking and being merry. I ate it all. My feet were tappin' to the music as the dishes mounted up. Patatas bravas, shrimp croquettes and spicy chorizo, before the main dish of paella. Jesus wept – this place was definitely a shirt-unbuttoner.

Claire turned to me and warned, as I made a pig of myself with the various tapas, "You better pack it in. You know what happened the last time you ate like a pig!"

"Jesus wept. Leave me alone. I'm on me holidays!" I retorted, then shouted over to the waiter, "Hey, Pedro. Ashtray and uno double Irish coffee, gracias, Señor!"

The double Irish coffee topped off the earlier beers and food very nicely. There's nothing better than ending a good meal with one of Ireland's finest. It's the perfect finish. But little did I know, this day was going to be more eventful than I had anticipated.

After I gave it the "Pedro – la cuenta, por favor," Claire nudged me and said, "Hey! You'd better go to the toilet before we walk back to the hotel!", but I wasn't having any of it. "I've already been this morning. You're worse than my friggin' mam, goin' on all the time! Give the man a break!"

On the way back to the hotel and beaming with satisfaction, I turned to Claire and said, "Deeew. We'll go back there again next time we come. Shame we're goin' home tomorrow!" We were only 200 yards down the street. My flip-flops were dragging on the pavement as Claire pushed the buggy. There was then a loud rumble – but sadly, it wasn't thunder.

"Is that your arse? You better get back to that bar. I told you this was gonna happen, you dirty b*stard!!"

There I was. In the centre of town, 200 yards from safety with both barrels fully loaded and the shotgun was about to go BANG!! I knew it was too late – there was no way I was gonna make it back to the restaurant. I was about to blow. This was gonna be another friggin' disaster. I was on the main high street of Calpe, with my arse against the wall. "Claire! Get the towel out!" I begged, and then the tsunami came. Wave after wave. Tapas after tapas. My arse was squealing like a pig. I wouldn't have liked to be the Spanish Eddie Yeats, having to clean that up in the morning.

I'm ashamed to admit that we used Iwan and his pram as cover. As several tourist buses went past, I caught the eyes of a lady, who nudged her husband and pointed towards me. I know she knew I'd shit myself.

"Ohhh, fuck!" I said to myself.

"Stupid bastard. Your own fault – the amount you've shovelled into you!" Claire went on. Once again, the local cuisine had ignited my irritable bowel syndrome and put me in another compromising position.

I whipped my shorts off and draped the towel around me like a Greek god. But make no bones about it – I wouldn't have got into heaven, the state I was in. I needed a good pressure washer – never mind a poxy shower!!

Once again, a pair of soiled Ocean Pacifics would be left as evidence. Claire was NOT impressed. I'll never forget walking the walk of shame back to the hotel. That mile felt like ten as I shimmied along the pavement. Thankfully, there was no ducker in the lift on our way back up to the room.

Thunder also struck in Jamaica. It was a slightly different story and sensation, to say the least. I was in Montego Bay and agreed to rent a surf-bike off a Rastaman. They were basically surfboards that you sat on like a bike and pedalled around on. He gave me a scabby lifejacket, fist-pumped me and said "Yeah man – I like your eyes. Like a fishman, Bob Marley style. Relax, mon!" Everywhere I went on that holiday, the Jamaicans loved my eyes.

It was a glorious day – not a cloud in the sky. There wasn't a ripple in the crystal-clear Caribbean Sea. So off me and my pal went. We spent a good half an hour pedalling about and admiring tropical fish like stingrays and barracudas.

We weren't far from the shore when lightning struck. I shouted to my friend, "Ohhhh, Daz – I need a shit, mate! It's that jerk chicken. I've been twice in the night!!" Daz had been a good pal of mine for years and he knew: if I had to go, I had to go NOW!

The only way out of this one was to fall into the sea and take a dump. I shifted my weight to one side and capsized the surf-bike. It didn't take much effort to relieve myself. I was bobbing up and the sea was no longer crystal clear as last night's jerk chicken and spicy rice clouded the water. I glanced over to the beach and noticed the Rastaman entering the waves. It's a good job I wasn't drowning 'cos he wasn't in any rush. I think he was more interested in his surf-bike drifting away. By now, I was trying to escape what looked like decomposed chicken bones, but it kept following me.

"You OK, mon?" he asked, as he swam up to my side. He then clocked the floating algae. I'll never forget the look on his face. "Ahhh – you relax too much, mon!" he laughed. "Get out before the barracuda get you!"

When he said that, I swam like fuck back to the shore.

C'mon lads, you can't tell me that I'm the only man that's ever shit himself in a foreign country. Is it the weather? Is it the change of diet? Or simply the fact that I always overdo it?

We've all done it!! It's a well-known fact that people in the building game carry a slop-bucket in their vans. Many a time I've heard Buzz shouting at me after he's got back in the van to find half a dozen pages of the *Auto Trader* missing. "You shit in here? It stinks, Trout! You'd swear there was a dead bird in here!!"

Look, lads – you'd all be lying if you said you hadn't been caught short a few times.

CHAPTER 6

Life's Little Pleasures

Football focus

I first started catching the odd footy game in the mid-Eighties, when I was about 10. Back then the stewards at Wrexham would open the gates of the famous Kop stand before the end and it was a good way to catch the last 20 minutes or so without having to pay a penny. But football wasn't really on my radar as a young lad. I was too busy ducking and diving. Don't get me wrong – I caught a few of the magical European Cup Winners' Cup ties in the Eighties. I had a paper round at the time, so I had a couple of quid to spend. The paper round soon ended though, when I got rumbled for dumping the papers down the allotments.

Around this time, Wrexham weren't exactly firing on all cylinders. It was usually bad, really bad or really duckin' bad! If I didn't have enough money to go to the game, I would be hanging around the window of the TV shop to catch the results on the vidiprinter. The vidiprinter was soon replaced by teletext. Oh, those glorious days of staring at the screen, waiting for that result.

And then it came. What a draw. Arsenal were coming to town. To say we were underdogs is a bit of an understatement: Arsenal were the champions and Wrexham had just finished bottom of the football pyramid. A classic David v. Goliath tie. I remember walking up Mold Road and seeing all the buses lined up. There was a real buzz in the air. I was there with a guy called Jim – my girlfriend at the time's dad, and a good bloke. He liked to drink. He'd sit on the settee after a long shift and think nothing of nailing a few Tennent's Super.

It's funny how strong the memories associated with certain sporting events are. I've got a memory like a friggin' goldfish and can't remember what I did this morning, never mind yesterday. But that FA Cup tie is seared into my memory forever. I was wearing my Reebok shell suit. Jesus wept – that thing was never off my back. It was a fantastic game of football and I'll never forget the look of fear and shame on the faces of Tony Adams and the rest of the team as they legged it off the pitch afterwards. That game will always be remembered as one of the biggest upsets in football history. That magical free kick from Mickey Thomas usually gets all the repeats, but we mustn't forget it was a local lad – Stevie Watkin – that got us the winner.

We stopped at the Spar on our way home and swilled a couple of those Tennents when we got back. You certainly couldn't overdo it on Jim's ale or last night's dinner would be making an appearance in the kitchen sink. Me 'n' Jim were buzzin' while we watched Wrexham on *Match of the Day* that Saturday night. The legendary Tony Gubba commentary will forever be remembered in Wrexham folklore. That was nearly 30 friggin' years ago and I remember it like yesterday!

You're not in Wales now!

As I look back on my times following Wrexham AFC, some matches bring me fantastic memories, while others I want to forget. Then there were those that were a mix of good and not-so-good memories. In the early Nineties, Wrexham drew West Ham in the FA Cup. That gave us a classic away day at Upton Park. I made the journey with some older lads in a minibus and drank my weight in ale on our way down to the big smoke – in those days, it wasn't that hard! It was a glorious day on the piss... We must have christened every motorway services on the M1. Anyone that's been cooped up, necking a few beers, will know the amount of piss-stops needed: once you pop – you just can't stop. Jesus wept – talk about the duckin' racehorse goin' for it.

It's a miracle we even got there. There was a boozer on the corner of the ground. We went in. I was a nervous wreck after hearing about the reputation of some of their naughty lads, and I sank a few swift ones. There I was, stood in the boozer, nine and a half stone soaking wet, wearing a knitted jumper which displayed the Welsh dragon. I'd loaned that jumper off one of Buzz's friends, begging him to let me borrow it: "Please, Doug. I'll look good wearing this. I might even get on the telly!!" In the boozer, I was too scared to go to the toilet, so I held it in for when I got in the ground. We supped up and went for a mooch.

When we left the pub, we noticed the Wrexham team coach. I erupted with drunken excitement. The excitement didn't last for long, as I was abruptly bought banging down to earth by a local copper.

"Take note of your sarroundings! You're not in Wales now! Count yourself lucky it's me that's got ya rawnd the throat!!" he shouted as he slammed me against the wall.

Deeew – he'd come out of nowhere. Looking back, he was doing me a favour. I was quite shaken up. I looked down, and my alky jeans were well and truly christened.

'Ahhh fuck – I should've gone for that piss!' I thought.

I'm sure I wasn't the only Welshman staggering around saturated in piss that day. It was a cracking game and with just a few minutes left on the clock, Steve Watkin was put clean through. At that stage it was 2-2. We all knew this was it. We were going to do some more giant-killing. It was going into the top right-hand corner. Then suddenly – from nowhere – the Hammers' number one flew through the air and palmed the ball to safety. It was a draw, but it still felt like a win for us. I didn't go home

At Wembley with Bobby

Beers in Taylor's Tavern, watching Wales in the Euros

Bore da from the working man's pit

Owen Glyn Davies' take on the Captain

Debating the
gameplay
with
Wrexham
diehard Eryl

Cheltenham
races with
the legend,
Irish Marty

Christmas jamas arent just for Christmas!

Cosmopolitan Wrexham

Don't give the Flamethrower any duckin' ideas!

Cooped up like a chicken at Hyde

Down at the Brave Nelson in Essex with the boys

Duckin' about on the canal

Euro fun up at the Working Man's Villa

Football and beers in the sun at Rhyl FC

Ernie in his P for prick hat!

First birthday party at the new bungalow

Good times on a Wrexham away day

Hazel showing her approval

Harry Potter is hanging out of his arse this morning

He shoots, he scores! At the Camp Nou

If you can't beat 'em, join 'em, says the Flamethrower

In the Mumbles with the Romanellos

Interviewing the King of the Kop, Jacko

It's not all beer, fags and football, you know

Livin' it large at the Working Man's Villa

Livin' our best lives

More beers at the Beachcomber with Dave

Lookin' dapper

MILAN PARIS NEW YORK GWERSYLLT

with the lads on the minibus – they were going on the prowl. So I blagged a lift back from some blokes from Johnstown. I was home for *Match of the Day*, but sadly didn't see myself in the Welsh Dragon jumper.

Anyway, a few days later, Buzz's mate wanted his jumper back. I took it round and was mortified to find out there was a big fag burn, the size of a golf ball, in the back of it. Jesus wept – I must have had friggin' Kojak jumping all over me after that Wrexham goal. Deeeww – the size of that singed hole was some sight. Buzz's pal played hell with me about it.

That East London adventure was one of my most memorable away days.

It's not always about the win in football. We went on to lose the replay 1-0. In all honesty, I was more interested in going out gallivanting with my mates in the Nineties and doing what young lads do. Apart from the famous FA Cup runs, I was seldom seen over at the Racecourse.

My passion for watching live football didn't really kick in until Wrexham had been relegated out of the football league. Prior to this, my main consumption of footy was on the telly down the Wheatsheaf. Sundays were indeed Super and Wednesdays were just as good. Wednesday night was Euro night and that would normally involve having a few cheeky tokes of rocky over at the bus stop at half time, only to return with eyes like Satan. Tony, the landlord, knew the score, but at least we weren't stinking the pub out. The place really used to be bouncing in them days. The curtains would be shut and the lads would be packed in like sardines as we watched the epic battles of Keane and Vieira.

Wired up

After a few years of keeping my head above water, the building game slowed up and work got scarce. I'd had a couple of dead-end warehouse jobs that had lasted only a few weeks each and then a good friend of mine, Dean, managed to get me a start at a wire factory. I'd become disillusioned with the ups 'n' downs of being self-employed and embraced the idea of stability. It was a half-decently paid job and you could always top your wages up with a bit of overtime.

When I went for the interview, I noticed a few familiar faces and they all said, "If you get a start here, make sure you don't end up on machine 14 or 15!" Lo and behold, sod's friggin' law, I got the job and ended up working these dreaded machines. Before my arrival, these barsteward machines had broken many a man. It didn't take me long to realise that I was doing the worst job in the factory. It was tough, and it was also dangerous. But I was determined that these bastard things wouldn't break me. I had a few nasty accidents... I even burnt my pecker on the red-hot wire. The shop floor had two furnaces on it. That was great during the winter months, but Jesus wept – in the summer you'd be beaming. I used to dread having to go to that place in the summer. I used to call it

Tenko after the Japanese prisoner-of-war camp series.

At the wire factory, you'd work four on and four off. The 12-hour shifts were gruelling. My life was mapped out before me by the Calendar of Doom stuck on my fridge door. Initially I enjoyed the routine, regular pay and paid holiday – but after a while, the cracks started to show. Before long, I was a regular in the shift manager's office, as I was prone to a few outbursts. After a couple of years, them machines were beginning to break me.

It was around this point that I started taking a keen interest in the trials and tribulations of Wrexham AFC. Everyone who works shifts knows that the run of days off is glorious, but the clock's always ticking and pretty soon it's payback time. Going back to work, I'd always feel depressed. But looking back, I know I was lucky to have had employment and the wages were certainly better than I'd been used to. With a few extra notes in my pocket, I was able to afford to follow Wrexham playing home and away more often.

Going to the football was a way for me to let off steam after being cooped up in that factory for an eternity of 12-hour shifts. Without those blowouts, I would have been on a murder charge. Claire was still a permanent fixture but didn't have a problem with me going to the games.

Back then it was a case of 'work hard, play hard'. During the last hour of every shift, I'd be planning my estimated arrival time at the Wheatsheaf pub with my mate Dean. Those first few ales used to go down a treat after being stuck in Tenko for 48 hours. We'd both be slurring our words after a few pints. I'm not being funny, but 12-hour shifts are too long. No one should have to work that long. It was like a friggin' death sentence! I felt like I was on death row – clocking in at six in the morning, knowing I wasn't going to be clocking out until six at night. At the end of my shift, I used to run out of that place like it was on fire!!

Hitting social media

In about 2009, while still at the wire factory, I started ducking about on social media. By now, Facebook was the main form of escapism. I opened an account with a profile pic of myself sprawled on a catamaran off the coast of Lanzarote. The cyber world was engulfed with pictures of shit dinners and the ins 'n' outs of Tracey's social life. My newsfeed was soon swamped by scrounging skip rats who wanted something for nothing:

"Anybody got a van I can borrow?"

"I'm after a TV (40 inch or above)!"

"Know a cheap plasterer who won't let me down?"

Jesus wept – Facebook seemed like it was full of nosey barstewards. Gone were the days of curtain twitching. You only needed to fire up your laptop to see if Susan had managed to get a doctor's appointment.

I took to Facebook like a duck to water. I'd post regular updates of my crappy Sunday lunches and led people to believe that 'Café Avenue' was a genuine establishment.

"Where is this café, Karl?" a friend would ask.

"Fully booked this week, I'm afraid!" I'd reply.

Back in the wire factory, phones weren't allowed on the shop floor. But nobody took notice of that rule – every ducker had one. Even the shift manager! I was regularly to be found behind my machine, updating the cyber-community on how much pain the prison guards at Tenko were inflicting on me.

It doesn't sound like much now, but one crafty ducker could get Sky Sports on his phone. We'd regularly crowd around it to watch the big game while the wire piled up on my broken machine. Jesus wept, I think more wire went in the skip than in the warehouse. No wonder the place went bump!

After posting a few pics on Facebook, I tried out a few videos. I got some interesting comments, like, "There's something wrong with you" and "You're not right in the head!" – and I began to enjoy the banter. I then went on and opened a YouTube account. I started uploading videos like 'Cock with a wok' and 'Dude pukes after eating bugs in Bangkok'.

A torrid time in Thailand

Deeeww – Bangkok was an eye-opener. Claire and I had booked another far-flung trip, to Thailand. At this time, I was in touch with a bloke from London who me and a few of the lads had met in Greece. Allan was a solo traveller and we had some great sessions on the lash with him. When I told him about our imminent trip to Thailand, he liked the sound of our itinerary.

"Bangkok – Phuket – Koh Samui – Koh Tao – Bangkok. I like the sound of that circuit. Do you mind if I jump on with you guys? I'll do my own thing when I get over there and sort myself out," he said.

"Yeah, of course!" I replied, without bothering to consult Claire.

Before I knew it, we were all in a Bangkok. Allan was about 6' 5" – his legs were almost as tall as me. I'm sure he had a bit of Dutch in him. He wore a gold bracelet, white linen trousers, slip-on shoes and always had a Benson & Hedges on the go. One of his sayings was, "We 'avin' a couple of light ales, Karl? Get 'em in. I'm just gettin' sam smawks."

Allan loved a few light ales and always used to like finishing things off with "A couple of large Bacardi and Cokes, Karl!"

Deeewww – he liked his grub as well. We went to one place and had huge prawns. That evening, we drunkenly finished things off with fried insects.

"Go on – try a few. It'll be a right laugh!" Al insisted.

Jesus wept – I puked like Regan off the Exorcist, all over the pavement.

The following morning, the three of us flew to Phuket and I was still unwell. I had serious food poisoning.

"It's them fucking prawns we all had!" I screamed to Claire, in pain.

"I'm alright, and I had prawns. It's them insects you and Allan were eating!" Claire yelled back.

Deeeww – I was cooped up for 48 hours. Raging temperature one minute and freezing my nutsack off the next. And there was no sympathy off Claire: "Your own fault if you wanna act like a dick!"

After a few days, I resurfaced and was keen to catch up with Al. It turned out he hadn't done much sightseeing. He'd spent most of his time at a bar over the road, playing pool. While smashing a few balls, Allan had met the woman of his dreams.

"Met her last night. She's the bookkeeper from the local bar! Ya don't mind if she tags along with us to Koh Samui, do ya, Karl? We'll have a right laugh!!" he said.

Claire was fuming about spending her hard-earned money travelling around with two people she didn't know. Matters went from bad to worse when Allan kept trying to get me to go for a game of pool with him at his sweetheart's place of work. Let me tell you this: there was no Kung Fu Fighting there, but plenty of ping-pong.

"C'mon – you'll love it, Karl!" he insisted.

"I wish he'd fuck off! I can't believe you've done this to me!" Claire seethed.

"Jesus wept – I didn't know he was here on the friggin' pull, did I?!" I replied.

"And I know what he's up to, trying to get you to go to go for a game of pool!!" she went on.

I realised that I'd made a mistake. Bringing Allan along for the crack brought me nothing but grief. To be fair, it was wrong of me to expect Claire to appreciate the company of a man who'd screwed back more balls than Jimmy White.

To be honest, it took Claire and me a while to adjust to the Thai nightlife. While we knew the ways of the world, some of the establishments we saw were real eye-openers. Allan was definitely enjoying his holiday more than us. I was well aware that love could be found in Thailand, but quite shocked to see just how quick. In the blink of an eye, he'd found his soulmate and was going to woo her for the foreseeable future. He'd booked two tickets so they could follow us to Koh Samui.

"Us four are gonna have a right laugh, Karl!" he grinned.

'Jesus wept – Claire's gonna duckin' love this!' I thought to myself.

So off we all flew to Koh Samui, with me receiving some serious grief as the realisation dawned on Claire that she'd be spending the rest of her holiday watching Allan being hand-fed Thai oysters. Deeew – there was no way I was getting hand-fed anything except a load of grief. Years later, we returned to Thailand and I made sure there was no one else in our company to lead me astray.

A few months later, it turned out that trip had been a fruitful one for old Allan. He was to become a dad. Those oysters must have done the trick. I never heard from him again and often wonder where he's havin' a few light ales now. He was a good old geezer.... Wherever he is, I bet he's "'avin' a right laaaaugh!"

Making and editing videos

Back home in sunny Wrexham, I was still acting the goat on social media. I'd film it all on my phone and then spend hours back at Café Avenue editing the footage. I was enjoying my new-found hobby. After a few videos of just larking about, I went on to vlog my match-day experiences. My first was for a home match – Wrexham v. Cambridge. I uploaded the video and titled it 'Bootlegger MOTD'. It gained a bit of a cult status amongst the Wrexham diehards. Before long, I found myself interviewing various locals. "Your score predictions for today?" I'd ask. Common replies included "Fuck off! You're not putting me on it!" and "Who's this bellend?!"

Looking back, I probably did look a bit daft. But I duckin' loved it. I loved chatting to the fans and getting their score predictions. I'd pop up in various pubs and whip my phone out and interview a few locals before the game. A few pints later, I'd be behind the goal, anxiously trying to catch some match-day highlights while trying to keep my phone steady.

Behind the helmet

I started to really enjoy doing these videos. I got the knack of editing and embedding graphics. I really did think I was going to be Wrexham's answer to Steven Spielberg. I created different characters, like Bubba Ball Bag and Taffy. These where the main protagonists. But there was one character that didn't require so much acting. He was 'Bootlegger', AKA the Captain. The Captain would attend games proudly wearing the red Wrexham shirt and a brown leather jacket, which I christened 'The Italian Pigskin'. The Italian pigskin wasn't from Italy and I doubt it was even made of leather, but deeeww, the rain wouldn't half bounce off it.

By now, I'd be a regular face at the home games and I'd try my best to get on a few away trips. It was on an away trip against Gainsborough that I met up with a lad called Ian Selfridge. He was a big fan of the Bootlegger MOTD videos and my cult Italian pigskin.

"I've got something for you. I've got a gift to accompany your non-Mediterranean look," he said to me. So we met at a boozer before the match. I was a bit intrigued to find out what this present was and I was looking forward to meeting Ian. Ian had lived on a Greek island for several years and was a bit of a character. He was really supportive during those early days of uploading videos. So there I was, a few ales in, with the lads before kick-off. Ian walks into the beer garden, we shake hands and then he takes it out: the helmet. No, not that helmet – the helmet. It was a brown leather motorcycle helmet, with goggles. It matched the Italian pigskin bob on. He placed it on my head like he was crowning me. It was an instant hit and became a part of the Captain's persona. To this day, the helmet sits proudly on my mantelpiece. I'd never part with it. It tells the story of many a classic away day and has even been on the heads of a few Wrexham players, when they won the FA trophy at Wembley.

We lost to Gainsborough on the day I got the helmet, but made it through to the final at Wembley on aggregate. I caught a peach of a goal by Danny Wright, which curled straight into the top corner and sent the away fans into a frenzy of raw emotion. I'll never forget bouncing up and down with Colin from Harlech. Colin would later gain notoriety for his goal-line pitch protest at Kidderminster.

We were away at Kidderminster when the referee disallowed one of Cheesie's goals. It had gone in, and then out through the side-netting. Boy, did we let the referee know. It was pandemonium. I called the referee – a woman – a stupid cow at the time. It was an explosion of disbelief. That outburst didn't get me any fans with the women's lib brigade. Fair play to Colin – credit where it's due: he parked his arse on the touchline and it took a few stewards to remove him. With a long delay and a lot of protesting, the goal was finally given. I still get the piss taken out of me because of my reaction to that incident. But that's football – it can flip your emotions. It can make you feel as high as f*ck when you're winning, but it also has a habit of kicking you when you're down.

I'd only bring the helmet out for special away days. It didn't feel so nice squirming out of Wembley after the play-off defeat to Newport County. After the sweet success of the FA trophy win, missing promotion was a bitter pill.

Around now, my life seemed sort of normal, but the Calendar of Doom was grinding me down. Every time a mate asked if I could go anywhere, I'd check the calendar and I'd be on friggin' nights. But I always kept ace cards up my sleeve, like 'The bad back' or 'Ingrowing toenail fiasco', just in case Wrexham had a game on.

Following the football was always about having a good time. With non-league football, although the football on show usually isn't brilliant, it's always a great excuse for a glorious piss-up. Football rivalry aside, I've realised that there's a lot of mutual respect. It's more about the love than the glory.

Tenko 1, Captain 0

Back at the factory, things were going from bad to worse. The cracks were getting bigger and Tenko and the dreaded machines were turning me into a loon. I'd just enjoyed a three-week shutdown, living like a millionaire, wooing Claire with a trip to a Greek island. Before I knew it, my tag was beeping and it was time to go back to jail.

I begged Claire to let me pull a sickie but she was having none of it.

"Get to work. You've only gotta work two nights, you lazy bastard, and then you're off again!" she said.

I reluctantly took her orders and went to work. Wrexham Industrial Estate always has a whiff in the air. If it's not the cheap Polish fags, it's the rank aroma of microwavable lasagne.

I clocked in at 6 p.m. I was seething. After living like Peter Stringfellow for nearly a month, I wasn't in the right frame of mind for this shit. Anyone that's been on a shutdown will know that the first day back at work is a duckin' grueller. By 7.30 I was getting funny looks from Blakey, the tall, gangly shift manager, who was just like the bloke off *On the Buses*. He was giving me evils because he wanted my machine to go faster. I was on *mañana* time but wasn't in Skiathos now.

He shouted over, "14 should be purring by now!" That was like a red rag to a bull. I flew up off my seat. Maybe the fact that I was sat on my arse was enough to alert his Spidey senses.

I wasn't in the mood to take orders from anyone with bigger safety glasses than Deirdre Barlow! I answered back, "I've got one pair of hands! If you want them to purr – then make 'em purr!" By now, I'd gone over the edge and allegedly used some very crude language. Looking back, I didn't play my cards right. I should have just gone home with a sore throat.

"I'll tell you what, who the f*ck do you think you are?! F*ck you, Blakey – you're not on the buses now! I'm going home! Stick your job!"

Deeeww – I couldn't get them overalls off quick enough. I got back home and Claire's first words to me were, "You dickhead! What have you done?"

There was a long, drawn-out inquiry. I decided to represent myself. I felt like OJ Simpson as I walked into that inquiry, but I sadly didn't come away with the same verdict as OJ and it was most definitely me that got the bullet, baby. The glove was a perfect fit. I was deemed to have broken company policy and was relieved of my duties. Deep down, I knew that I couldn't have stayed there forever. The machines had won. I respect anyone who can do 12-hour shifts. No hard feelings to Blakey – I actually quite liked the bloke. It's just that the factory environment was too regimented for me. Once again, I was escorted off the premises, thinking to myself, 'Oh f*ck. Here we go again!' There were a lot of good lads who worked at that factory. They tried to help me, but I was too proud and stubborn to take their advice.

Doing what I'd done that evening was really selfish. Mainly because we'd not long bought the house. Well, to tell you the truth, the mortgage was in Claire's name. My credit rating had more holes in it than Rambo's pants!

"I'm not working for you to sit on your arse playin' FIFA. You better find a job. We haven't paid off that Visa card we used to pay for Thailand yet!" Claire fumed.

After a few ales down the Wheatsheaf, I made the announcement. "The roofer who's scared of heights is back in business!"

Buzz wasn't in the roofing game any more, so I was on my own. I called myself KP Roofing. I got myself a T-shirt with 'KP Roofing – you'd be nuts not to use us!'

I did alright. Work was sporadic. I'd work for two weeks and then be off for three. Two weeks' work every month was enough to keep afloat, but Claire would often raise hell if I was lounging around the house in my undies while she was working nights in the cheese factory.

She used to dread coming home after a long night shift, wondering how many waifs and strays would be spangled on the settee. It couldn't have been nice coming in, expecting to go to bed with a cup of hot chocolate, and finding a group of rigger-booted lads sat round listening to Hot Chocolate.

Back on the roofs, I was doing OK. I wasn't breaking any records, but I was keeping my head above water. I was my own boss. If I wanted an early dart, I would most definitely have an early dart.

It was around about this time that the flames ignited between myself and Claire, every time she found out I was calling for a couple of quick ones on my way home from work. Jesus wept – she was telepathic. As soon as I walked into the pub, my phone would start ringing. One thing was for sure – I wasn't picking it up. But she was always one step ahead of the game and would have

clocked the van there. The early darts were the perks
of being self-employed and those midweek beers were
a necessity to keep the working man sane. At the time,
we had a liberal relationship. With no children, the only
responsibilities we had were to pay our bills and look after
Hazel.

Shaggy dog tales

Hazel was a liver and white springer spaniel that we'd
bought as a puppy off Buzz. She was no bigger than
the size of my hand when we first brought her home.
We treated her as our baby and she lived a glorious
life, reminiscent of Joan Collins. I loved Hazel. She was
a very excitable soul who would get a bit carried away
sometimes and piss all over the laminate when you'd give
her fuss. You'd always hear me shouting, "Don't stroke
the dog!!" to whoever was calling over... Then I'd be
fuming as I mopped up another pool of piss.

We'd regularly take Hazel for walks down the river.
She used to love a good swim. I was at the riverbank
one day, throwing stones in for Hazel, and I bent down
to take one particular stone up. As I tried to sling the
supposed stone, it disintegrated in my fingers. As a bloke
would, I looked at the remaining fragments and smelt my
fingers. 'Arghhh, fuck – that's dog shit!' I thought, as I
let out a silent scream. It's weird, I never minded picking
up Hazel's poo, but picking another dog's crap up used to
wind me up.

This leads me on to the story of the Phantom Shitter of Gwersyllt. For weeks on end I'd return home from work, bumping the van up the kerb and onto the drive. And every day, I'd find a huge mound of it in the middle of the drive. It was like something off *Groundhog Day*. I knew it wasn't Hazel's. Jesus wept – you'd swear there was an orangutan living in my hedgerow. Over a period of time, this constant shovelling of someone else's shit began to grind me down. I was desperate to find the culprit.

Then one day when I was cleaning the back of my van out, I turned around and there it was before me. The Beast of Bodmin: a huge German Shepherd, curling one out on the drive. I threw a trowel at the dirty bastard. I was glad to have caught the offender and relieved it wasn't one of the locals.

I gave chase and saw it run into a house nearby.

"It's always getting out, that bloody dog! It went to the toilet in my garden the other day," I heard one of the neighbours shouting.

I legged it back to the scene of the crime and shovelled the evidence into a carrier bag.

'Jesus wept – it shits like Chewbacca!!' I thought.

With a steaming bag of dog shit, I marched up to the culprit's house. The whiff of it was making me heave.

I knocked on the door. She didn't answer to start but I could see someone moving about in the front room. She couldn't hear me knocking 'cos she had Status Quo blaring – 'Rockin' All Over the World'.

After a few more knocks, she came to the window. She opened it.

"Hello! Can I help you?" she said.

"Yeah, you can. Is that your dog?" I asked, through gritted teeth.

"Yes!" she replied.

"Here you are, then!" I replied, handing her the bag.

"What's this?" she asked, expectantly.

"Don't get too excited, love. It's dog shit. Your dog shit!" I said, with satisfaction.

There she was, standing in her front room, open-mouthed, with a carrier bag full of freshly laid turf that King Kong would have been proud of. Poetic justice! I never saw that dog again and my drive was to be a safe haven. I was once again free to wear my Jesus sandals on my own drive.

Trevor's taxi

Although I was living with Claire, I was regularly left to my own devices and one weekend ended up on a mad one in Manchester. Me and a couple of pals had got tickets to see Robbie Williams at Old Trafford. We had a damned good go of it and were in glorious form. At the height of euphoria, I was listening to Robbie belting out 'Mr Bojangles'. I then went walkabout. The next thing I know, I'm on a packed bus, hanging on to the handrail 'n' thinking to myself, 'Where the hell is this bus going to?' At the first stop, I made a dart for the doors and got off. God knows where I was – to this day, I still don't know. I saw a car parked up, opposite a chippy.

"I need to get back to Wrexham, mate. How much?" I asked the driver. He was a small African man.

"You give me £80, bro, and we be OK. Wrexham is a long way!" he said. I only had £20 and a bit of shrapnel in my pocket, but was sure I'd be good for the rest once I got home.

I gave him the usual taxi blag. "You been busy tonight, mate?"

"A man's gotta hustle!" he replied.

"What's your name, mate?"

"I'm Trevor. I'm from Lagos!" he replied.

Once we got on the motorway, he turned his stereo on. When he slammed it into fifth gear, I realised he meant business and was in just as much of a rush to get home as I was.

"You wanna smoke, bro?" he asked. By chance, I had enough for a scabby one-pop.

'Deeeww – this is the taxi driver sent from heaven!' I thought. Then I looked around his car and realised that this was no duckin' taxi.

Ultimate awareness then took over my senses. The closer we got to base camp, the more uneasy the mood felt. It was now time to come clean with the driver and explain I only had twenty quid on me.

"You fuckin' with me, bro?!" he raged.

"No – I'll just need to nip in and get some extra money," I explained.

By now we'd peeled off the motorway and were on the old Summerhill Road, which is a dark country road leading to Gwersyllt. I started panicking as I realised I didn't have any money back at the house. I was praying that Claire would be in. He turned to me and in the dark, all I could see were the whites of his eyes.

"F*ck me, bro. Where do you live? You run on me and I'll kill you!" he warned. There was no chance of me running anywhere. I was well and truly with the marshmallow man. I had eyes like saucers and legs like Mr Soft. As we reached our house, I prayed that the lights would be on.

"I'll be good for it!" I slurred. My Plan B was waking up the old lady next door. My heart was racing.

Thankfully, as we came up the drive, the lights were on. Jesus wept – I've never been this happy to see the missus. But with what was left in her purse, we were still £15 short. Luckily Trevor was happy to be on his way with a couple of pouches of baccy.

I spent the next hour soaking in the bath. F*ck knows what had happened to me when I was on that bus. But whatever it was, it didn't smell nice.

Once again, I copped a load of grief off Claire. I most definitely laid low for a few days after. Every time I listen to 'Mr Bojangles' now, it makes me f*cking cringe.

Looking back, I was lucky. That could've been a totally different scenario if it hadn't been for Claire.

Trev – if you're ever in Wrexham, call into the Wheatsheaf. I owe you a drink or two.

To be fair, the ol' Flamethrower isn't as bad as I make her out to be. She lets me have a fair ol' crack of the whip and has been there for me a few times. We've had more laps than Nigel Mansell and more ups and downs than Den and Angie. After 20 years plus, our love still burns profusely like an unlit fag. I'm lucky that she's not one of these girls that is obsessed with tying the knot. Though come to think of it – would you want to walk down the aisle with me? I know what you're thinking – 'Duck dat shot!' You wouldn't want my beady eyes whispering to you, "I do!" We're both of the opinion, 'If it ain't broke, don't duckin' fix it!'

CHAPTER 7

Things Get Tasty

Nothing to declare

I'd been grafting on the roofs. I was never one to follow protocol regarding the correct attire. I was often spotted wearing an old pair of Bermuda shorts, which more often than not had a big rip in the arse. With legs like a pair of turkey drumsticks and odd socks, I was a sight to behold. I've been pulled a few times for wearin' the ol' Adidas on the job, but those daft duckers don't understand – I can't walk on a roof in steel-toecapped beetle crushers.

Claire was working 12-hour shifts and I was having busy stints followed by a period of layin' low. The layin' low was sometimes involuntary – it was the nature of the beast. Anyone that's been self-employed will know it's not always a bed of roses, and you're only ever a few weeks from being a sinking ship.

It was the beginning of October, 2014. I was stuck in a rut with no work and duck all on the horizon workwise. I was 39 years old and skint. "You're always friggin' skint!" Claire would say. "Funny how you've always got money for the pub and football though, innit?" I was on the bones of my arse. Then one morning a big brown envelope came through the post. Sadly, this big brown envelope wasn't full of £50 notes. I took one look and my heart sank. My guts began to bubble. "Oh, f*ck! This is off the taxman. Hang on it's worse – it's off Customs and duckin' Excise!!"

I ran to the toilet for a quick dump and thought to myself, 'I bet this is something to do with all those fags I tried to bring home from Goa!!'

I read the letter and my Spidey senses were spot on. Six months previously, I'd been pulled to one side in Manchester Airport after returning from Goa. I'd foolishly taken some bad advice about the amount of tobacco I could bring back. Looking back, maybe Matt from Derby wasn't the best person to be asking advice from after a few Kingfishers in the Bending Bamboo bar.

I'd bought 6,000 ciggies and honestly thought I was fine to go through the Nothing to Declare gate. Me 'n' Claire split them 50/50 to make life easier in terms of packing. We went through passport control and towards the stairs by the luggage carousel. I looked towards the luggage area and the place was swarming with customs officers. 'Fuckin' 'ell – they must think Pablo Escobar was on the plane,' I thought. After a 10-hour flight, I looked like Beetlejuice and the last thing I wanted was any aggro off these duckers.

I turned to Claire and told her I was going to the loo and would meet her outside. Then as I stood waiting for my case, I noticed the people off our flight getting pulled left, right and centre. My arse began to twitch. I was on one side of the carousel and Claire on the other. I then noticed this bloke whose piercing gaze was fixed on me.

'It's about to get friggin' tasty!!' I thought.

The second I walked over that Nothing to Declare threshold, I was pulled to one side off the same bloke. Seconds later, Claire was pulled too.

"Are you travelling with this lady, sir?" he asked.

"Yes!" I replied.

"Why have you walked through separately, ignoring each other?"

"I've just went for a dump, mate!" I replied.

He told me to unzip my case. He had a good old rummage through my rancid clothes. No wonder he needed to wear a pair of gloves. That was embarrassing, but nowhere near as embarrassing as when he asked me to open the hand luggage. We opened our bags and there was enough ciggies to keep Bet Lynch goin' during furlough. He laid 30 sleeves of Lambert & Butlers out, just like they do on *Banged Up Abroad*. Deeew, I was sweatin' like f*ck.

"You're 28 sleeves over your allowance, sir!" he said.

"But that man in the airport told me I'd be OK – it's the same as Turkey!" I protested.

"No. And because you're so much over your limit, I'm confiscating your limit as well!" he announced.

I began to seethe. He took all the fags and said, "I'm not going to fine you, but one of you will need to have this matter stamped on your passport!" He wouldn't even give me a pack of 20 for the journey home! I signed the declaration and let him stamp my passport.

Fast-forward six months. I'm stood in the back kitchen and this letter tells me that I owe fourteen hundred notes in duty. Apparently, I was picked up in an internal audit for having signed a declaration for 30 sleeves in my hand luggage. I rang the direct line and tried to explain that it was all an innocent mistake, and that I'd only had half the amount they'd stated.

"The bastard's already had my fags, for f*ck sakes!"

After a lot of grief, I managed to get the fine down to six hundred. However, it was still a kick in the ball bag to the workin' man who wasn't workin' much.

To this day, I still always get a wry smile from the officers as I walk through passport control.

A nice surprise

So, there I was: I'd thought I was skint before – but after that brown envelope arrived, I was really duckin' skint. After that unfortunate mistake, I had to get a credit card so I could pay another duckin' credit card – it was a real nightmare!

With my 40th birthday looming, I began to think, 'I'm gonna have a right shit birthday!' I was on Skid Row.

It was the beginning of October and I'd been moping around the house. Claire came home from work and said, "I've got a surprise for you!"

"I better rinse my nutsack!" I said.

"No, you dirty bastard. I've booked Barcelona for three nights, for your birthday!" she said.

Fair play, Claire had been saving over the previous few months. I was a bit embarrassed, but quite excited too. It took a few seconds to sink in. I'd never been to Barcelona before. In all our years together, that was most definitely the most romantic thing Claire had done.

Before we left, she warned me, "This time, you won't be bringing any bloody fags back!"

Barcelona is a fantastic city. You can go on a cultural tour or you can enjoy the beach. I found myself slumped on the beach, enjoying the autumn sun. Deeeww – there I was, a pale Welshman, lying on a Bob Marley beach towel 'cos I'm too tight to pay for a sun lounger. Even though it was October, the sun was shining and the weather was good. I needed to get some sun on my white skin. I was paler than a rizla.

At the hotel reception there were fliers for the upcoming Barcelona v. Ajax match. Without hesitation, Claire went and bought us a pair of tickets for the Camp Nou encounter. Deeew, this was turning into a proper away day.

"Are you wearing that to go?" she asked me as we left for the stadium. I was wearing the Wrexham home shirt

– long sleeved. I sweated my knackers off in that top, but I was determined to patriotically show off my hometown club in such a famous European stadium.

Those Catalans were switched on: they clocked the Wrexham top as soon as I walked in, and gave us a warm welcome. In my mind, I felt that coming from Wales, I had a Gallo-Romance thing going on with my hosts. Whatever, one thing was for sure – those Catalans like the Welsh.

"Gal·les!" I'd hear them say.

"Sí, Señor!" I'd reply, in my best Spanish.

We'd had a few swift drinks on the way to the stadium, so by kick-off I was well and truly lubricated and ready to get some footage for my MOTD blog. The thing was, our seats were up in the sky with the gods, so the players looked like ants. There was one thing for sure, though – you could spot Messi a mile off. I was gobsmacked at the pace of the game – it was a sight to behold. As the pitch was too far away, I took to filming the crowd – "Don't put me on it!" Claire seethed. So I filmed a few of the Catalans, and they were willing participants. They must have thought they were on some sort of Jeremy Beadle thing.

"Hey, Miguel – who the hell is this?" they must have been sayin'.

Jesus wept, those Catalan pensioners were probably wondering which hospital I'd escaped from. It was a pulsating Champions League tie. Barcelona won 3-1.

Neymar scored, Messi scored, Ramírez scored and a few hours later, following one or two *cervezas*, the Captain scored. Then along came Iwan. I wanted to call him Messi, but Claire wasn't havin' it. "You're the only messy Phillips in this house!" It was a romantic break, made even more memorable by the fact I didn't cack my pants for once. Maybe the tide was turning.

While waiting for Iwan, I did a lot of thinking. I suppose most fathers do this. 'I'm gonna need to up my game, baby. I'm gonna have an extra mouth to feed!' I'd think to myself. In the back of my mind, I knew that my life was gonna be a whole new story with this little person around. No more dancin' under the coconut tree or winter trips to Goa.

I won't lie: I was very excited. I think my excitement was obvious for everyone to see. I was also cautiously concerned with the thought of suddenly being expected to grow up at 40.

Nine months soon went and Iwan was born. After the birth, Iwan and Claire needed to stay in overnight. I did what most fathers do: I went straight to the Wheatsheaf and got absolutely blasted.

It was a special and weird time. I found myself at the end of the garden havin' a rollie rather than waftin' my smoke by the patio doors. Looking at a small child makes you realise how vulnerable we are. I began to worry and started to wonder, "How am I going to make all these pieces fit together?"

At 40 years old, I was a mature father. A lot of my pals had had kids in their late teens. It dawned on me how much they'd sacrificed in their younger years while I was away with the fairies.

The Newtown job

There was now four of us at Café Avenue. One minute I was pickin' up Hazel's poo, the next Iwan's. Jesus wept – I'd dealt with enough shit of my own over the years, and now I was up to my eyeballs in a someone else's. I was dealing with more shit than a linesman.

By now Iwan was skiddin' around the house on a baby-walker like a possessed Dalek. His new habit was testing my patience by opening and closing cupboards. I bought a load of those cupboard latches, but then I couldn't open the barstewards. Deeew, this Daddy business wasn't as easy as it looked. There was no more *Corrie* or *EastEnders* on TV – he wouldn't settle until he'd had a fix of *In the Night Garden*. Jesus wept, that used to freak me out a bit. Some of the characters had bigger eyes than me. How the hell he used to sleep after watching the psychedelic antics of Igglepiggle, Makka Pakka and the gang is a duckin' mystery!

At this time, I started to actively seek more graft and things began to pick up. I met a bloke called Martin Hough, who ran a local building company. He had some work going in Mid Wales – Newtown. It was initially only meant to last a couple of weeks, but one job led to another and it was a long stint. I was working with a bloke called Geoff and we had a shitload of work for us to clack at. Geoff was an old-school joiner. The roofs that we needed to do were a piece of piss for him. We were a good team: he'd build 'em up and I'd be behind him, whackin' the roof on. We were earning some good coin for once. I knew this wasn't going to last forever because Geoff was in the process of selling his house and wanted to emigrate to Canada. I liked him – he swore a lot. It wouldn't take much to set him off on a swearing spree: "Look at these c**ts!" "Look at this dozy bitch!" "Have you stolen my lighter, you thieving fucker?"

Those early-morning drives to Newtown were duckin' gruelling. It sometimes took over an hour, depending how many friggin' tractors you got stuck behind. It was a boring, mundane drive, but quite scenic in parts. We had nothing to do but smoke. Geoff was an exceptional smoker. He'd chug away like a steam train.

"F*ckin' hell, Geoff. Open the window. I can't breathe in here!" I'd say to him.

"You open your window. You're smoking too!"

We'd go at it hammer and tongs, arguing about who smoked the most. Anyone who was driving past would've thought the van was on fire. The toxic combination of Geoff's Polish fags and my Golden Virginia overcame me on one fateful afternoon.

"I've had enough! I can't f*ckin' breathe. That's your sixth tab and we're not even in Oswestry yet!" I shouted.

"Counting, are ye! Crafty bastard. With your driving – I'm a nervous wreck every time you go round a fuckin' bend!" he bellowed back.

"My eyes are stingin' – I can't fuckin breathe!!"

"If you don't like it, find your own way to Newtown!"

So that was that. The next day, we went in our separate vehicles to Newtown. No wonder the emissions levels were off the scale. There was now two smokin' chariots hammering it through the Welsh countryside.

After a few days of sulking, we were back in the van together. It's funny how you fall out with your workmates over trivial things. Two grown men, arguing about who had the worst smoking habit.

We were like George and Mildred. We spent more time together than we did with our partners. We both loved the early dart. He always liked to call in for a few on the way home… and a bet on the gee-gees. There was just one problem: Geoff had the sense to go home after a couple but I didn't, much to the annoyance of the Flamethrower. My tea would be going 'ding' in the microwave!!

I miss Geoff. He's in Canada now – smokin' his head off, no doubt. Deeew, we had some laughs.

After Geoff left, I continued the contract with a pal of mine – Rich. After clocking nearly 20,000 miles in 12 months, the van was more knackered than me. Things soon came to a head with it. With an early dart on the cards one day, we downed tools and decided to shoot off. At the first junction, the van made a loud clunking noise.

The gearbox was shot. I couldn't get the ducker out of second gear. We hadn't reached Welshpool and we had three miles of traffic behind us. With those narrow roads, it was impossible to overtake us. Every time a car did take a risk and manage to pass us, they'd hoot their horn and flick the 'V's. I would then return the rude gesture. Jesus wept – that was one fun ride home!

On the move

Our little stint in Newtown gave me the chance to put a few quid in the sock drawer towards a new home for the family. We bought a bungalow. I'd always wanted a bungalow – no stairs to fall down. As luck would have it, a guy down the Sheaf was selling one in just the right spot. He was playing on the bandit and harping on about how he'd had enough of the area. I thought to myself, 'No wonder he's had a gut full of it around here – the amount of money he's ramming in that bandit!'

Once again without any consultation with the Flamethrower, I told Mike, "I'll have it!"

I was buzzing. It was only a small place, but it was on a corner plot and there was plenty of scope to extend. We sealed the deal while Mike was still playing the bandit. He ducked off to Fuerteventura and it's nice to know that he eventually found love there. We all miss Mike, but I don't think anyone misses him as much as that bandit down the local does.

Nadolig Llawen from the Captain

Golwg
Cyfrol 33 . Rhif 15 . Rhagfyr 10 . 2020

"DIM FI
YDY'R CAN
MWYA'
CŴL YN
Y FFRIJ"

holi'r Capten sy'n
seren ar Twitter

Cau bwytai a
thafarnau yn
"ergyd go-iawn"
i bysgotwyr

Y Cymro sy'n
ffilmio'r Tŷ Gwyn

Glyn Sgrech
- yr Adferwr sy'n
caru ei fro ac yn
gweithredu ynddi

Never did I think they'd want my mug on the front of a magazine!

Oh, what a beautiful morning!

No Country For Old Men up at the Villa

On the terraces

Out with Len, treating the ladies!

Pre-match beers before the first game of the season

Poker night at Len's

Slightly overdid it!

Steak night with
the brewery lads

Super Sunday
with Parry

The Captain, illustrated perfectly by Mark 'Sparky' Davies

The legend that was Mark Jones, AKA Sarge

The lovely Hazel

The Martian has landed

My toxic trainers

Doin' the walk of shame in Calpe

The extension takes shape – I'm proud to have good mates!

There's one thing I don't mind humping, lads

Unfounded optimism down at Wembley

Who else would you invite to open your hairdresser's?

Who let the Dougs out?

With Brett Johns, MMA fighter
extraordinaire

Out with Josh from Wrexham Lager

The long-suffering
Flamethrower

My sister from Ireland pays a visit

With the family for Iwan's birthday

With The Sherlocks

Work hard, play hard!

Working up a thirst in Llanidloes

Yes!

I'm not a big fan of bandits. I find the friggin' things anti-social and I've witnessed a few tortured souls blowing all their wages on a Friday afternoon. These days you need a master's degree in engineering to work them out. Duck dat shot, I'd rather back a horse.

We left Café Avenue with a tinge of sadness. The place had held many memories. But it was time to move on and create a family environment. We were only moving around the corner and the Wheatsheaf was still within walking distance. We moved into the bungalow and it soon dawned on me that we needed more room. I started to get on the Flamethrower's nerves and Iwan was ramming into my toxic trotters.

Toxic trotters

The toxic trotters first made an appearance on the island of Lanzarote. I'd foolishly worn my trainers with no socks, and after a few days, there'd be a strong, strange smell. It got worse in the evenings.

"It's something to do with the drains!" I said.

"It stinks of shit!" Claire confirmed.

"I'm gonna go to Reception and play f*ck about this. It's like livin' on a sewage farm!" I seethed.

That evening, me, Iwan and Claire went for a meal down the harbour. Halfway through the main course, Claire says to me, "Ughhhh – I can smell it again. It smells like our hotel room!"

We got back to the apartment and I was well oiled. I took off my trainers and got myself a can of San Miguel out of the fridge. Next thing I know, Claire's screaming like a banshee. You'd have sworn she'd seen a rat.

"It's your trainers – that's what the smell is!"

On closer inspection, we discovered that it was indeed my feet that were the problem. My trainers were humming and I'd been diagnosed with toxic trotters. The only cure was to buy a pair of Jesus sandals from the Moroccan at the bottom of the hill.

"Those trainers have gotta go!" the Flamethrower insisted.

"I'm not throwing them – they'll do me for work!" I said. So we agreed to put them out on the balcony.

Cue 7 a.m. the next morning. I'm havin' a smoke on the balcony and I can hear the couple next door.

"What the f*ck is that stink?" the woman goes.

"It must be those bloody bins round the back!!" he replies, as I creased up with silent laughter.

The following evening, around 6 p.m., I looked down from our balcony and saw a guy fumigating the entire area. Whether this was something to do with controlling the cockroach population or he was trying to neutralise the stench of my toxic trotters, I'll never know!

I'm sure I'm not the first and not the last to suffer from this unfortunate ailment. At the end of the day, there's nothing a quick squirt of Lynx Africa can't sort out.

If the worst comes to the worst – blame it on "the bins round the back!"

Party like it's 1999

Back at the bungalow, I got the ball rolling with the extension. But I needed to pay for it and that meant more graft in Newtown. Just like Geoff, Rich was also critical of my driving.

"My life flashes before me every time you corner a bend!" he'd say, as he chuffed away.

"Jesus wept – someone else that's not happy with my driving. Whassa matter with yew lot – for fuck sakes!!"

It was 2019 and those Friday early darts became a thing of beauty. Sometimes I wonder if it was worth driving there on a Friday at all. There was nothing more refreshing than rinsing the ol' nutsack and then having a cold pilsner. Rumour has it, I've even been known to have a pilsner while rinsing the nutsack. Everyone should try it. Just don't drop it, baby.

Once showered and clean, you'd often find me swilling in the back kitchen – which was actually a front kitchen. Work that one out! I loved it – those golden hours, the house to myself. Iwan would be at his Nana's on a Friday night, and Claire would be at work. This gave me the green light to let rip. I bought a draft machine, which became known as the working man's kettle. I would regularly get blasted and post my antics to social media.

My modus operandi was to spin around on the spot while informing everyone about the gruellin' week I'd had.

I'd enjoy having the back kitchen pounding to different tunes, from Kenny Rogers to the theme tune off *Minder* – I loved it. Listening to those TV theme tunes would make me reminisce about the good ol' days at my grandparents'... It's weird how music can transport you back to good times. The back kitchen Fridays were notorious!

2019 was full of good vibes. My social media following was on the up and by Christmas time I had a few bits of merchandise out, like cups and even a Christmas jumper. It was quite bizarre to think that my ugly mug was on someone's morning cuppa in another part of the country.

Towards the end of 2019, I decided to participate in Stoptober to raise money for Macmillan Cancer Support. I moped around for a month with a face like a smacked arse. I'd glance over and see the Flamethrower devouring a glass of vino tinto.

"Drinkin' again, are ye? You're like an alky!!" I'd shout.

She loved watching me suffer that month! As the weeks went by, I'd get people saying, "I bet you feel like a million dollars, Captain!"

"I'll be glad when this shit's over!" I'd reply.

The people backed the Captain and in the end I raised just shy of eight grand. I was proud of myself for managing a whole month of sobriety, but there's no way I'm doing that again!!

Around this time, The Fat Boar in town did a spoof beer to raise a few extra notes for charity. With my rising social media presence, the idea of bringing out my own pilsner was bandied about. Towards the end of 2019, the dream started to take shape. Several meetings later, the deal was done. The Captain was gonna have his own pilsner, brewed by the legendary brewery, Wrexham Lager.

Since Iwan arrived, Claire and I hadn't had much time with just the two of us. Not that I'm complaining. By now he's five years old and developing his own personality. He's quite an inquisitive soul. "Where you going now, Karl?" he always asks when I'm on my way out. I don't know why he calls me Karl – I don't know where he gets that from. "Karl!" he shouts, when he wants something.

At the end of 2019, we went on a trip to Scotland. Just me, Claire and a few friends (Lenny, Daz & the Damsels). Glasgow turned out to be very different to what I expected. The Scots were up for the crack. It was in Glasgow that I heard a booming Scottish voice: "Hey you, Captain – I'm gettin' you a drrrrink boy. And ayyeee – I'm buyin' ye pals one too!" This dispelled the myth that Scots are as tight as a gnat's arse. It also made me realise that I'm not only known around Wrexham.

While trying to get into a bar in Glasgow, a bouncer asked, "How much have yeee had to drrrink today, boy?"

"Not enough, baby," I replied. He appreciated my wit.

"Take your time pal – we're watching ye!" he replied, with a friendly smile.

CHAPTER 8

The Plague Years

An expensive mistake

2020 wasn't off to a good start. I'd had a monumental session down the Sheaf and finished things off in the back kitchen. The Flamethrower was away so the cat most definitely played. One pint led to another. Next thing I know, I'm goin' for it with half the local building site. There was more high-vizzes in that back kitchen than there was in the local cop shop. Jesus wept – we drank the house dry and even managed to get some carry-outs from the Sri-Lankan off-licence. By 2 a.m., I'd crossed the Rubicon... and wanted to go on. Duck knows what time I reached my pit. All I know is, when I woke up, I was still in my work clothes. I felt a damp sensation. I got up to put the kettle on and noticed I'd been lying in three gallons of recycled pilsner. 'Oh, f*ck!' I thought. 'I won't be able to blame this on the cats!'

The mattress was saturated in piss. It was only six weeks old. The strange thing is, my alky jeans were dry! Work that owt! I must have got out of bed and, instead of takin' ten steps to go to the pan, slashed all over our luxury pocket-sprung mattress like Red Rum. I almost remember doing it. I remember the oozing relief of emptying my bladder.

The Flamethrower returned. She was fumin' from the minute she walked in the door.

"This house stinks of fags!!" she raged, and when she saw that the kitchen looked like I'd had an after-party with The Rolling Stones, the flames roared stronger.

"No one's been smokin' in here!!" I shouted back.

"They've been stubbin' out their fags in the sink!" she shouted. "You better get in 'ere and clean it. God, it stinks!!"

She then stormed into the bedroom. Granted – the kitchen was a mess, but nothing a mop, a bucket and a bit of bleach wouldn't sort. But I knew there would be no easy remedy for the predicament I'd got myself into in that bedroom.

By now, I'm hunkered by the patio doors, nervously puffing on an Amber Leaf. In all the awkward situations that I'd ever been in, there'd always been a way out – even if that meant running. But there was no place to run. There was no place to hide. I had to face the music. There was an awkward silence, and then it came – the Flamethrower in all her glory. She was about to explode like an atomic bomb!!

"I can't believe it!" she erupted. "You're 40 years old!! It's you that needs the nappies, not Iwan!"

To be fair, the place stank like a cat sanctuary.

"You've ruined it. You daft bastard. You're gonna have to buy a new one – I'm not paying for it!!"

"No, I won't. I'll get your mum's carpet cleaner. It hasn't soaked through. We'll just turn it over!!" I offered.

"No – we're gonna need a new one!" she insisted.

That glorious piss-up down the local ended up costing me more than an arm and a leg. There's nothing worse than workin' all week and then havin' to shell it out for duck all. All because I couldn't hold my ale. I was treadin' on eggshells for quite a while after that episode. There was no sign of Ronnie Wood and the lads for a few weeks. And whilst layin' low in the doghouse, I faced the shame and embarrassment of having to buy two mattresses within six weeks. I didn't hang about in the local tip when I dropped that ducker off. You'd swear Peter Barlow had been kipping on it for 20 years.

That bedroom incident was a bad omen. 2020 hadn't started well. But I was determined to soldier on and put it down as a lesson learnt.

Getting it up

After months of feeling cooped up within the four walls of the bungalow, we finally had the green light to go ahead with the extension. I had a mate of mine called Daz building it for me. Deeew – Daz didn't mess about. I'd be lying in my pit, and the mixer would religiously crank up at 7.30 a.m.

"C'mon, Dodge! Get that mix on!!" I'd hear Daz shout to Dodge, who was working with him. You'd see the veins pumpin' in Daz's neck and he looked at you as if he was gonna drop the nut on you.

Jesus wept – he was like clockwork and he ran his jobs with military precision. I soon learnt not to offer him a brew before the regimented times.

"I TOLD YE – half past ten and half past twelve, Doug!!" he reminded me a few times. At the 10.30 break, poor Dodge would struggle to get through a full fag, never mind a butty and a quick piss.

I admired Daz's work ethic. He was on the job at the crack of dawn and didn't have time for small talk.

"I haven't got time to talk shit to you all day, Doug. Where's that mix, Dodge? I want it here – NOW. And I want this mess cleaned up. C'MON!" he'd bark.

Dodge had a knack of working with a fag in his mouth without all the smoke goin' in his eyes. The only problem was, Daz never gave him a chance to take a drag from the ducker. His fag would regularly disintegrate into ash without him enjoying a single puff.

During lunchbreaks, we were discussing current events. The rumour was, there was about to be a lockdown.

"Aye, Doug! We better get all the materials before we go into f*cking lockdown, or we'll be f*cked!!" Daz warned, grimly.

Daz was on the ball. We did go into lockdown.

I'll be honest – I didn't take it that seriously. As the sun shone, I was more than happy to top up my tan with a few cold ones in the back garden.

Around this time, the Bootlegger Pilsner launched. With most of the country housebound, the brewery started to see the orders coming in.

Fair play, the lads soon carried on working on the extension again. Talk about bein' on-site mornin' till night. After a while, I got used to the schedule: I knew that when I was halfway through watching *Homes Under the Hammer*, it was time to do my bit and put the kettle on.

20 days and 20 nights had passed and the Trojan had built the extension and handed it to me to do the inside and the roof. I'm most definitely not foreman material, so the rest of the work took me a bit longer, to say the least. It took me five months to think about putting the poxy windows in. I kept on reminding the Flamethrower, "Rome wasn't built in a day!"

I dread to think how many bottles of pilsner I swilled while talking a good job with a few mates. The days turned into weeks and the weeks into months. It was like friggin' *Groundhog Day* staring at those breeze blocks.

Being self-employed, the bank was reluctant to lend me any money. So, due to events beyond my control, things were paused. Passers-by would often shout as they went past, "Hey – it's comin' on now, Doug!"

I'd shout back "Comin' on? Duck all's happened for the last two months!"

"You'll get there in the end!" they'd reassure me.

Deeew – they were right! Slowly but surely, things started to pick up. With a few slabs of Bootlegger to offer, I was able to tempt a few tradesmen over. By the summer, the Bootlegger Pilsner was getting a great reception. It was quite surreal seeing blokes up and down the country swillin' the Captain's brew.

Things began to get tasty. They always say, "Don't get high on your own supply!", but I was guilty of committing that crime. The cha-ching of the empties hitting the back of the bin waggon was like Mike dropping the jackpot on the roulette machine. But that's what happens when you need to bribe tradesmen.

Irish Marty

Irish Marty – now there's a man that didn't need much bribing. Deeew – me 'n' Irish Marty put the world to rights a few times in the back garden while the extension was taking shape. He'd often turn to me and say in his Irish accent, "Aye, she's beginning to look like a home now!" after putting one or two boards up.

"A home – more like a refuge!" I'd reply.

"Yew jest wait till yew get a bit of skim on her!" he'd smile back.

Come November and it was time for the plasterers. Jesus wept – those guys were animals. They came to look at the job on a Friday afternoon and made a good dent in my booze stash. It's a good job I had a few friends in the brewery trade. The Flamethrower chucked them out at the stroke of midnight, but was there to greet them with a bacon butty in the morning.

"I'm getting out of the way of you lot... just don't get HIM in a mess!" she warned, before duckin' off to the Working Man's Villa.

As soon as Claire's Clio was off the drive, we were back on it. It was my job to make sure everyone on site was looked after. That was one job I was quite good at. Some pals had a business: Kegs on Wheels. They set up a bar in the hall. It was a good job Claire had gone away because that day turned into a right grueller. By teatime, we were all ducked and well on the road to Tipperary. We were back on the blower with Kegs on Wheels. "We're gonna need another keg!"

We all ended up in the back kitchen, bobbing about on the spot, dancing to a bit of Kenny Rogers. Kenny always gets 'em goin'. The problem with having to work on the Sunday is, you've gotta know when to hold 'em, but I didn't duckin' know when to fold 'em.

I woke up in a terrible knot. I lay in my pit, asking myself, "I wonder if those duckers will turn up to finish the job?" Part of me was hoping they wouldn't. They did. Credit to them – I couldn't be arsed. I looked and felt like death warmed up. But they were ready to go first thing in the morning. Ten to nine, I could hear Lenny swearing in the garden.

"C'mon, open the fuck up Doug!" Jesus wept – that man could swear.

Those lads were obviously made of sterner stuff than me. If you'd struck a match near me that mornin', I'd have flown into the air like a firework.

These days, I often sit in the extension, look around at their handiwork and chuckle to myself, reminiscing about that legendary weekender! We took it to the limit and it was definitely worth it. From Irish Marty to the plasterers, Alex the electrician to Danny the plumber and Dindo the painter, the lads got me over the finish line. Maybe I could crack it as foreman after all.

The Working Man's Villa and podcasting fun

You've probably worked it out yourself. I don't actually own a friggin' villa – it's really a static caravan! But that duckin' caravan's been a home from home. Iwan loves it. I love it too. And as long as the Flamethrower is happy then I'm going to be happy. I love an early dart on a Friday and hittin' the road to get to the Villa.

There's nothing I like more than having a break over at the ol' Villa, whether it's veggin' out with an old James Bond film or getting blasted in the Beachcomber – even if my patience is tested by all the noise that Iwan and his cousins are makin'. It's worse than a zoo. No wonder I'm drinkin' so much.

Deeew, that sofa in the caravan is rock hard, but I can often be found stretched out on it, snoring like a pig, halfway through *Match of the Day*.

I never thought I'd be into this caravan lark, but I kinda like it. Don't get me wrong – it's not all rosy. With my toxic trotters and morning antics in the bog, I cop a fair bit of abuse. The Flamethrower can often be heard screaming, "It stinks! Open the windows!" But the smell soon disappears once I get the frying pan out and rustle up a legendary fry.

I've featured the ol' Workin' Man's Villa in a few of my videos, but it had its own feature-length episode during one of my podcasts, which went out in the summer of 2020. The podcasts were fun to make, but I didn't feel like I was ready to invest so much time in them. Logistically, it wasn't possible to travel so much, and believe me – I don't like the sound of my own voice enough to hear myself blagging for over an hour. Having said that, Gareth and Alex – who ran the podcast – put a lot of graft in and I'm sure they'll go on to bigger things.

One thing's for sure – if it hadn't been for the podcast, I wouldn't have had the pleasure of spending a memorable afternoon with my footballing idol: Mickey Thomas. Apparently you should never meet your heroes, but I wasn't missing this for the world, baby. They say the sun always shines on the righteous and it was most definitely true on that splendid afternoon. It was beaming, baby. And the fridge was fully loaded. I loosened up with a few pre-match pilsners before Mickey T got there. And then he arrived. He looked like a million euros in his tight Armani jeans. He put my sock 'n' flip-flop combo to shame. He must have taken one look at me and thought, 'What the duck have I got myself into?!'

He had some great tales to tell for the podcast and some even better ones off the camera. The man was a genius on the pitch and a man of the people off it. I bet he was some character in the dressing room back in the day. After the podcast and before he left, he gave me some words of advice. One nugget of wisdom came when he took a look at my rancid chariot and said, "You see that heap of shit there. Don't ever change it. You are who you are and the lads love you for it. You're a legend!"

"No," I replied, "you're the legend, Mickey!"

And off he drove into the Prestatyn sunset with a slab of my pilsner on his passenger seat. What a superstar. I'm still waiting to kick his arse on the golf course. I think he's frightened of my six for four, for two, baby!

Doing the podcast also led us to a memorable wide-eyed night out in Essex. Gareth and Alex sorted out a gig with London boy Tom Skinner. I was quite apprehensive about going down to Essex and meeting the bling boys, but let me tell you now – I was well looked after. We filmed it at The Brave Nelson and I was welcomed with open arms. I'd gone down with Josh and Ali from Wrexham Lager and as we'd just been released from lockdown, we were determined to go for it. We didn't get much sleep that night, baby. Jesus wept, we hadn't even started filming and we'd already had six or seven Italian pilsners each. I'd been following Skinner on social media for a while before we met, and I knew he was a bit of a lad. When I met him in person, it was refreshing to find out how down to earth he was. Boy, could he get it down him. By early evening, even on a Monday night, that boozer in Brentford was bouncing. Fair play to them – they showed us some decent southern hospitality.

We had a good crack at the podcast, but it wasn't to be. My plans of being the next Terry Wogan didn't quite work out. That's what life's about – some things pan out and some things don't. You never know till you try. And if you get knocked off your horse – you gotta get back on it and ride again, with no two flying ducks given.

Moretti killed the radio star

Speaking of things that didn't work out, there was the time I was given the opportunity to go on national radio with Robbie Savage. I'd been told several times over the years that I have a face for radio, and this was my chance to shine. Wrexham AFC were on the verge of a massive takeover and footballers Robbie Savage and Chris Sutton wanted the Captain's opinion. The phone rang about half ten in the morning and Robbie briefed me about what they were gonna ask. When I told Robbie I was at the Villa, he said, "Whatever you do – don't get bladdered this afternoon, Captain!"

"Don't worry mate, I'm layin' low this afternoon!" I reassured him.

I hung up and looked at the clock. It was only twenty to eleven and the show wasn't on till early evening.

'I've got ages to go until I do this, and my arse is already bubbling!' I thought. So I went into Prestatyn to lay my Saturday afternoon acca down the bookies. Jesus wept – I should have just set my £20 note on fire because yet again, I was on a losing streak. You're meant to bash the bookies, but they seem to have a habit of bashing me, more like.

As I walked up the High Street, I looked through the windows of a bar and noticed that the footy was on.

'Deeewww – that'll do me! I'll just have a couple while I watch the game!' I thought.

In the back of my mind, I heard Robbie's voice warning me: "Whatever you do – don't get bladdered this afternoon, Captain!"

Those couple of light ales turned into a few. One to two, two to three and then I was past the point of no return. I was well and truly beaming, but convinced myself that a cold shower and a few coffees would sort me out. Once again, I'd slightly overdone it. By chance, Claire was driving past Prestatyn High Street and clocked me necking my seventh pint of Moretti. She tooted her horn. She looked angry.

"You better sort yourself out. You're on the radio in a bit. You'll make a fool of yourself!"

She wasn't wrong. It was showtime and the phone rang. I wasn't exactly on form. It was to bed I should've been goin', not on national radio.

I was like Phil Mitchell on New Year's Eve. Those Morettis had more than calmed my nerves – I was like a rabbit in the headlights. Out of nowhere, I had an uncontrollable bout of the burps. I ended up sounding like Toad off *Wind in the Willows*.

Robbie immediately smelt a rat. "You been out this afternoon, Captain?" he asked.

"I have indeed!" I replied, with an extra burp for good measure.

"Sounds like you've had a good afternoon, Captain!"

The next day, when I rose from my pit, I realised that I'd let myself and Robbie down. Nerves had got the better of me. In hindsight, me doing an interview on a Saturday evening had the ingredients to the perfect shit sandwich. Anybody who knows me knows that I don't normally lay low on the weekend.

Kiss my putt

That last episode almost brings us up to date. My main distraction since then has been this book. Since having Iwan, I've realised that time is the most valuable commodity a man could ever wish for. All jokes aside, I think I was a bit naive when I accepted the job... I honestly didn't think it would take so long.

Having said that, I've got a bit more time to churn up a few fairways as I work on my horrendous golf swing. Apart from playing John Travolta in the school play, my only other claim to fame was being crowned the Division 3 knockout champ at Old Padeswood Golf Club in 2010. Don't let that mislead you into thinking I'm any good at golf, though. I would regularly hear people calling me a 'shanker' behind my back – at least, I hope that's what they were calling me!

But for once, luck was on my side as I slowly but surely slayed my elderly opponents and made my way to the final. The combined age of the other competitors would have taken you back to the Jurassic era, but how the duck did I make it to the final? I must have hit all the trees on the par 5 and lost more balls than Dirk Diggler.

On Final Day, I'm up at the crack of dawn, trying to hit golf balls on the field. It didn't do my confidence any good, though, 'cos I was shankin' 'em, toppin' 'em and duckin' missing 'em completely.

'Duck dis shot – this is too early for me!' I thought.

At least I'd loosened up. I went home for a bit of bacon and egg and then headed to the golf course. On my way there, I must have smoked about four rollies. I got to the club in good time.

'Deeeww, if I can nail this today, my name's getting engraved on the board, baby. Up there forever. Amongst the other legends,' I thought as I looked up at the previous winners on display.

With 20 minutes before teeing off, I headed over to the putting green to tune in my beady eyes. So, there I was, waiting for the next elderly victim to arrive – and was gobsmacked when I realised he was the same age as me.

"Are you Karl Phillips?" he asked. My heart sank. 'This bastard looks like he can hit a ball... Deeeww, and he's got all the gear. Brand new hat, too!' I thought.

And boy, could he welly it. The thing is, the poor ducker couldn't keep it straight. I know it's not golf etiquette, but deep down I was buzzin' my nutsack off every time his ball went AWOL. To be fair, he was a good golfer once he got off the tee, but on that day, he was struggling. He was going here, there and everywhere bar the fairway... and the damage was done before we were on the dancefloor.

Hole after hole, I had the wise words of my mentor pal Alex ringing in my ears. "Slow back – follow through... slow back – follow through!"

As we got to the 14th tee, I had one hand on the trophy. If I survived this hole, the title was mine. I got my ball down the middle. It was one of those spawny grass cutters – I was just relieved to get it past the ladies' tee and goin' in the right direction. Then it was his turn.

I stood back and watched my opponent address his ball. He went and spannered it and I knew it was all over. The title was as good as mine. I couldn't contain my excitement. As he turned around, cursing, he caught a glimpse of me pointing to the sky like Diego Maradona scoring the World Cup-winner. I got a six and he got a seven. I'd only gone and won it. I couldn't wait to phone Alex. I think he was as proud as I was.

"How the fuck did you manage to spawn that, Doug?!"

The gods had most definitely smiled down on the Captain on that joyous day. I was a proud man as I sank a few pilsners and told every ducker that came into the clubhouse that I was the champion. I phoned every number in my phone and told 'em, "Ayeee – Division 3 knockout champion, baby!" before hanging up!

I was crowned champion and presented with my trophy, which reminded me of an egg cup. I'd have slept with that egg cup that night if they'd let me.

The following week, I couldn't wait to get to the golf club and see my name engraved on the champions' board. I went into the clubhouse, looked up and what an absolute friggin' disaster! Just my duckin' luck – they'd spelt my name with a 'C' instead of a 'K'.

I guess the moral of the story is 'Enjoy the moment'... it could be someone else's name shining under the lights tomorrow. And please – try not to laugh at the misfortune of others.

Enjoy life – and let the good times roll. Be good, and if you can't be good... don't be duckin' bad, baby!

OVER AND OWT!!!

Epilogue

An epilogue's where you're meant to comment on the ending. It's the conclusion. The thing is, though, I'm only in my late forties and becoming a father in extra time has made me realise that I need to calm down a bit (only a bit, mind!). So hopefully I've got another book in me before I reach the ol' back kitchen in the sky.

I was lucky to be offered the chance to write this book and I've tried to give it my best shot. When life throws any opportunities your way, you need to grab 'em while you can. They say 'God loves a trier' and I tell you what – I love 'em too. I've got a lot of time for anyone who tries to make things happen. I admire anyone that's got a bit of fire in their belly.

An electrician once said that I'm definitely not wired up to the fuse box. I would probably agree. In the world we live in today, being different isn't a bad thing, but I was written off by so many people over the years. I'll admit I've been no angel…. While I've learnt the hard way, I've got no regrets. I've made plenty of mistakes over the years, but let it be known: some mistakes are worth duckin' making. Like it or lump it – you need to experience the sour taste of defeat to truly enjoy the sweet smell of success. We can't change the past, but we can have a major influence on the future.

The world is most definitely changing. Things are a lot tougher for the youth of today. As a proud father, I'm finding myself giving advice. Seriously – do you think I'm the best person to be giving advice?

All I want is the best for Iwan and Claire. Claire has most definitely stuck by me through the good, the bad and the tasty times. I'm still known to test her patience. Deeeww – we do have our ups and downs, but I can always broker a peace deal with one of my legendary halloumi burgers.

Recently, I was told by a bloke in a pub, "You better prepare for the fall, Captain!" I looked him in the eye as if I was the Glaswegian bouncer, and replied proudly, "Well, I won't fall very far, 'cos my feet are well and truly on the ground – where they've always been, Captain!"

Acknowledgements

I'd like to thank Mickey Thomas. When Y Lolfa told me that he'd agreed to do the Foreword I was over the moon. Now that I've finished this book, my main goal is to improve my handicap and hopefully share a round of golf with that living legend.

I'd like to thank you, the reader, too. If you've made it this far, I'd like to reach out and shake your hand. Finally, I'd like to thank all at Y Lolfa, the publishers. This book has truly sent me to a state of insanity. To say it's driven me to drink is an understatement.

...and it's given me a serious dose of Japanese Knotweed!!

Karl Phillips
March 2022

Also from Y Lolfa:

£9.95
Autobiography of Wrexham FC legend Dixie McNeil.

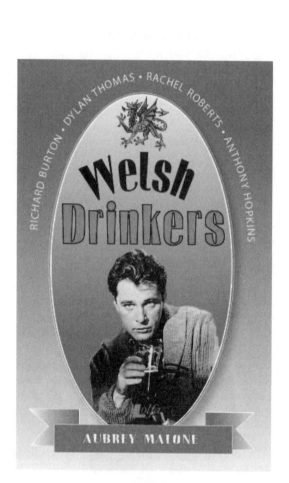

£4.95

Hilarious anecdotes about four of Wales' most infamous tipplers: Richard Burton, Dylan Thomas, Rachel Roberts and Anthony Hopkins.

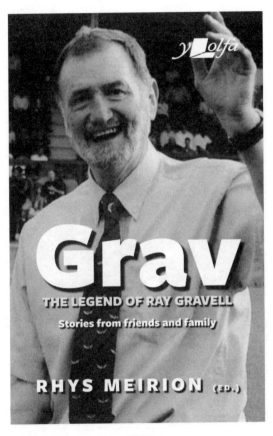

Grav

THE LEGEND OF RAY GRAVELL

Stories from friends and family

RHYS MEIRION (ED.)

£7.99

Touching and humorous anecdotes about Ray Gravell,
undoubtedly one of Wales and rugby's greatest characters.

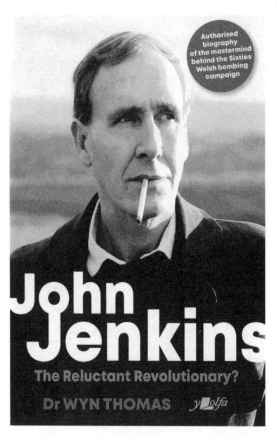

Authorised biography of the mastermind behind the Sixties Welsh bombing campaign

John Jenkins
The Reluctant Revolutionary?

Dr WYN THOMAS · y Lolfa

£12.99 (pb)
£19.99 (hb)

Authorised biography of Wrexham's John Barnard Jenkins,
Welsh nationalist and activist and one of the most
iconic figures in recent Welsh history.

£4.95

Light-hearted, fully-illustrated retro-style picture book to help
you learn north Wales Welsh with your furry best friend.

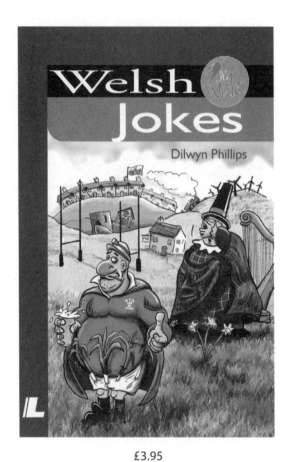

£3.95

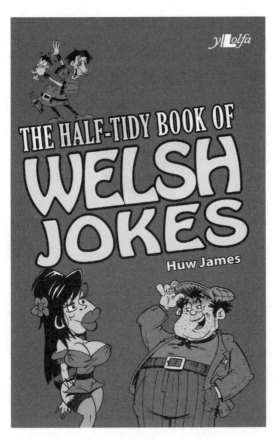

£3.95